EMELI
SANDÉ
READ ALL
ABOUT IT

EMELI SANDÉ
READ ALL ABOUT IT

JOHN DINGWALL

OMNIBUS PRESS
London / New York / Paris / Sydney / Copenhagen / Berlin / Madrid / Tokyo

Cover designed by Fresh Lemon

ISBN: 978.1.78305.357.5
Order No: OP55616

Exclusive Distributors
Music Sales Limited
14/15 Berners Street,
London, W1T 3LJ.

Music Sales Corporation
180 Madison Avenue, 24th Floor,
New York,
NY 10016,
USA.

Macmillan Distribution Services
56 Parkwest Drive.
Derrimut, Vic 3030,
Australia.

Every effort has been made to trace the copyright holders of the photographs in this book but one or two were unreachable. We would be grateful if the photographers concerned would contact us.

Printed in the EU

A catalogue record for this book is available from the British Library.

Visit Omnibus Press on the web at www.omnibuspress.com

Contents

1. MY GIRL

Adele Emeli Sandé was born in Sunderland General hospital, on March 10, 1987, weighing a healthy 7lb 4oz. According to her mother, Diane, it was a Tuesday when the newborn was delivered, and she could barely contain herself at the sight of her beautiful first child. Minutes later, while the baby cried for attention, Diane's husband, Joel, took her in his arms and soothed her, remarking on what a tuneful sound she made.

Joel was the musical parent of the two, or so he claims to this day, and there is little argument from Diane, who can barely resist the laughter as her husband light-heartedly takes what credit he can for his famous daughter's incredible success as a singer, recording artist and songwriter. It was after all, says Joel, he who played guitar and it was his record collection that was stacked with some of the finest R&B, soul, jazz and blues records ever made. A fan of Nina Simone and Aretha Franklin, it was Joel's love of jazz and soul that would have a huge influence on his daughter early on, when she became old enough to sing not just in the family home, but also in front of the general public at school and in talent shows.

Zambian-born Joel had met Diane while studying mechanical engineering in Sunderland, in the north-east of England. The Cumbrian town had played an important role in the UK's industrial past, but it was undergoing a transformation in the late eighties, as were so many urban centres up and down the country. Manufacturing had declined and the service industries were beginning to take over. But Joel couldn't put his education to good use in the UK even if the jobs were available for him to do so. He had been sponsored in his homeland and was committed to return to Zambia to work as soon as his studies in England were over. He took his wife, Diane, with him to Africa not long after the birth of their daughter.

In the months that followed, however, Diane – already pregnant with the couple's second child – fell ill with suspected malaria and returned to Cumbria to live with her sister. It was several months before Joel could join her back in the UK, whereupon they relocated to the tiny village of Alford, pronounced *a-ferd*.

Following the birth of Lucy, their second child, the pair eventually found work in Aberdeenshire, the thriving oil-boom city in the north of Scotland. Diane took a job with Aberdeen City Council and Joel found a teaching post at Alford Academy, where his easy-going manner endeared him to the pupils and proved a useful aid to their learning.

The only mixed-race family for miles around, they experienced the occasional incidents of what could loosely be described as racism, although the Sandé's generally play down any conflict they might have witnessed, and Joel insists that the north-east of Scotland and the idyllic Alford in particular was the perfect location to raise their young family. However, later, Emeli would admit she felt isolated at times and turned to music to express her feelings: "My song 'Mountains' is about their struggle, their journey and how we've all grown as a family."

Even before Emeli had begun to put her feelings into song, it seemed she was destined to be a singer. Joel and Diane would rush to her cot side at the occasional sound of their newborn daughter's crying, thinking her hungry or in need of a nappy change, only to realise they had made a mistake. Little Adele Emeli Sandé wasn't crying. Their precious daughter was smiling and, though she had yet to form her first words, she was making the most beautiful sound they could imagine, and it was then that Joel would turn to his wife and say, "She's singing."

Echoing her parents' assertion that Emeli sang even when she was in her Moses basket, Emeli's younger sister, Lucy, added: "There was a lot of music around, but I think Emeli had the music in her from the moment that she was born."

Even as a toddler, Emeli* shared Joel's love of artists such as Aretha Franklin, Whitney Houston, Alicia Keys and Nina Simone. "I remember when I was seven, even earlier than that, being three or four and just hearing these noises and not quite understanding what they were," she said. "I couldn't explain to my mum that I wanted to hear the same songs again. But at seven or eight, that's when I decided I wanted to be a musician."

Emeli recalls singing along to Mariah Carey's version of Badfinger's 'Without You', the song made famous by American singer-songwriter Harry Nilsson, whose version topped the charts in 1971. "I really loved Mariah Carey... I was about six and my dad came through and he heard me singing and he told me I was good," Emeli recalled. "That was when I was like 'I might be a singer'. He told me to hold on to the door to add dramatic effect. Thanks dad. My dad is very musical. He has a very good ear. He introduced me to a lot of music when I was young and that's how it all sparked off. My dad has some embarrassing stuff as well, but I took the good stuff. He introduced me to the album *Music Box* by Mariah Carey, and Nina Simone and other amazing singers. I was obsessed with Eternal. Then I started listening to radio late at night, different kinds of specialist music shows where I could kind of

---

* Emeli would be known as Adele until she reached her twenties, only then adopting her middle name, Emeli, as a stage name, after becoming aware of the success of another British singer-songwriter, Adele Adkins.

really get into the music and find out new stuff. I started exploring stuff when I was older."

The discovery of her love for singing led Emeli to take choir and recorder lessons from the age of six, at her primary school in Alford. Music teacher Morag Simpson is now justifiably proud of her most successful music student: "She was just a wee thing at that point," Simpson recalled. "She was known as Adele then. All the children had to play an ocarina, a South American instrument that is a wee cylinder with circles, and I taught her to play the recorder. She learned to read music. The recorder group, music-wise in primary school and nurtured in secondary school, helped develop her interest in music. She was a pleasure to teach and a delight."

Perhaps fittingly, the song that really inspired Emeli to become a singer is packed with the level of emotion for which she has since become renowned. 'Why? (The King Of Love Is Dead)' was written by Nina Simone's bass player, Gene Taylor, after hearing the news of Dr. Martin Luther King's death in April 1964, a day after the civil rights activist and Nobel Peace Prize winner's legendary "I've been to the mountaintop" address in Memphis, Tennessee, in which he foretold his assassination. Three days after King's murder, Simone sang 'Why?' at the NYCB Theatre at Westbury (nicknamed the Westbury Music Fair), New York City, in a concert dedicated to his memory (the performance was recorded and released as part of Simone's 1968 album *Nuff Said!*). On hearing this performance, and Simone's ability to convey heartfelt sorrow and yet be˙ uplifting, Emeli was convinced that her own future lay in music. She was just eight years old.

"Since I was really young I definitely knew I wanted to be a singer, but it was when my dad played a song by Nina Simone that I remember just thinking, all right," Emeli said. "I just felt so inspired by the song and I just thought this is what I really want to do. 'I want to learn to play properly and I want to be an artist.' Somehow I knew. It was like, deal done. I'm doing it. There was nothing else."

Emeli's sister, Lucy, recalled: "She was always a singer. Even before school she was singing Disney songs like *The Little Mermaid*. That was a particular favourite. She sang Mariah Carey songs that Dad had in his record collection. I remember the house would be filled with her singing all the big ballads. Those were probably the first songs she sang and I knew how good she was, even when she was just seven years old or maybe even younger … She would sing in the bathroom and the neighbours would complain or comment that they could hear her singing in the shower."

"I was always trying to write little songs when I was young so I remember my first proper song," Emeli said. "It had verses and choruses and I was really impressed. Everyone had to sit down and listen to it. That was about the age of seven or eight and the first song I ever wrote. I hope it got better slowly. Then I started playing piano when I was 11 so I was marrying the two things together. I was pretty young but I just knew. I played clarinet before piano. So I played clarinet, piano and cello.

From singing in her pram to singing in the shower, Emeli always had the music in her. There is some debate over whether she was in the Primary 6 class or Primary 7 when she took part in the school nativity play, *Hosanna Rock*, though Morag Simpson insists it was the former. What is not open to debate is that Emeli shone during a performance teachers still talk about to this day. She bagged the lead role and sang the title song. "We chose her for the lead role of Mary because we could see her talent then," says Simpson. "She had a nice soulful song to sing, which she did beautifully."

Headteacher Liz MacLeod said: "She had a wonderful voice and when she sang the song 'Hosanna Rock' solo, it sent shivers down my spine. On hearing a 10-year-old sing with such power and depth, everybody remarked on how special it was. Obviously, it was long before she became mega-famous but everybody was spellbound. It really was special."

Lucy admits her big sister's special talents paid dividends on occasion, particularly for the sweet-toothed pair whenever Halloween came around. "We were in the choir at the same time but it was always her that got the solo parts," she said. "But we would sing together in public at Halloween. We'd go round trick or treating and would sing a song. I was always the backing singer. We'd sing the songs we learned at school. We did quite well out of it."

Even in primary school, Emeli's songwriting talent was also beginning to shine. Those who witnessed Emeli singing at the Opening Ceremony of the London 2012 Summer Olympic Games, and saw a consummate artist, in control of her surroundings when performing to tens of thousands in a stadium at an event being beamed to billions around the world, would not be surprised to learn that this focus stretches back to her pre-teen life at home in Alford. Liz MacLeod recalls: "Emeli wrote a song for a talent show the children were doing. She didn't perform it. Her friends performed it for her. It is amazing that she was writing songs for other people even then."

Lucy said: "As a child Emeli was very good at making up games. She'd always be in control of what we were doing and singing. For my birthday, she wrote in the card this song we had written as kids. It was a really bad techno song we had created moves to. She wrote a few lines from it on the card. We also wrote a song on guitar as well, about a saviour who wasn't a fighter, but the techno one convinced us we could write songs, even though it is quite embarrassing. The main line was 'Techno is in the house'. We used to write songs and play at radio stations. Now it is inspiring to see her living her dream and seeing her do what she said she would. When I listen to the lyrics to a song like 'River', I think of her and how she has been such a good role model to me. When she was little she always loved music and performing on the recorder. When she got a little bit older and was in P7 or S1, I noticed that it didn't bother her getting up on stage. I could see the lyrics she was writing and how deep she was going into the songwriting by the time she was 13 or 14."

Joel said: "I knew when Emeli was six or seven years old that she had something special. From then on I realised she wasn't shy about making music. She tried to imitate the popular singers of the time and tried to get the sound the exact same as the records. She was standing in front of a lot of people from a young age. She was happy to be heard in front of adults. She would sing Celine Dion's 'My Heart Will Go On' and would try to reach all the notes. She sang Mariah Carey and Whitney Houston songs and later, at the age of 12, it was songs by Alicia Keys."

"I guess when you're a kid it's almost like a game where it feels like you have magical powers and can create things from thin air," Emeli said of her talents, "so I loved that and I loved performing the songs to my parents. My family is a big inspiration, especially my sister. My sister's younger than me but I do feel she's a lot wiser than I am. She's a big inspiration in my life and when I feel confused she definitely gives me clarity."

As far as Emeli is concerned, she owes her talent to family lineage. "My dad's family is very musical – they all just have the real ear for music. I've been writing letters back and forth and it's just amazing to find out I have all these cousins who are into music too – one's a piano player, one's a singer, and so on. [Dad] took the school choir when I was at school and taught himself how to play guitar."

Perhaps if Emeli had lived in Glasgow, one of the most thriving centres of commercial music in the UK, or Manchester, Liverpool or London, she would not have found the space to develop as a youngster. She may have been intimidated by the number of unsigned artists who see their hopes dashed on an almost weekly basis. Certainly, according to Emeli, Aberdeenshire – and in particular the small village of Alford – was the ideal setting for her to develop her talents. Without the distractions available to youngsters in many major cities, she concentrated on her music while other children her age involved themselves in pursuit of the park, playground and PlayStation.

"I'm really glad I grew up in Aberdeen and had time to develop the skills and sense of perspective I needed," Emeli said. "I found it very difficult at school to meet people, to make friends. I felt very different, so I spent most of the time writing music by myself. If you don't fit in anywhere, then there are no rules. You can do what you want. There is an upside to being on your own."

One upside being that she started to teach herself the piano when she was 11, with dad Joel's encouragement and mum Diane's blessing.

Joel was delighted when his daughter said she wanted to broaden her audience, and when she turned 12, he enrolled her in piano lessons in the Aberdeenshire town of Inverurie, a 35-mile round trip from Alford. Emeli's parents ensured her regular attendance at the hour-long lessons by ferrying her to Inverurie then heading into the town for some retail therapy while she learned her favourite instrument. On most occasions it would fall to Diane to drive Emeli for the weekly lessons.

Her teacher, Ian Milne, recalls: "She came to me for piano lessons for a few years from her last year of primary school … right up until her O-levels. In school holidays she would take a break, so it would be 35 to 40 lessons a year." Ian admits many of the children he taught were dragged along by their parents, so he was delighted to find a music student with a passion for learning. "She always wanted to know as much as possible about everything. She wanted full information. She was always a very enthusiastic and hard-working student when she was at school and she had a great interest in music. I knew her as Adele at that time. Of course, I am calling her Emeli now."

Emeli is perhaps best placed to explain where her dedication to study – not just music, songwriting and piano, but all the subjects on offer to her at school – came from. When she moved on to secondary school and Alford Academy, the same school her dad taught at, her focus became even more acute. "I hated to be ill and to miss a day because I was so hungry to learn. I was very shy, nerdy and extremely well-behaved. Inevitably, throughout secondary school, it was part and parcel of my identity that I was Mr Sandé's daughter. No way could I muck about or get into trouble, because it would've got back to him within minutes and Dad was strict, let me tell you."

Milne's love of jazz helped reinforce Emeli's passion for that particular genre, which, along with soul, comprised a large part of her father's record collection. "I have a great interest in jazz and chords," Milne said. "We did quite a bit of teaching on chords and she was very keen to learn all about that. As well as being interested in jazz chords, I was also interested in all sorts of other chords so, as well as the usual piano lessons, we worked quite a bit on chords and theory. She always wanted a very full understanding of that. It came across all the time that she had a thirst for learning. She also had a very good ear. She was born with a good ear, which is so important. That is a difficult thing to develop, and she had that naturally. I maybe gave her some of the theory behind it and gave her some help backing that up. Diane would listen to her practise every day and I would listen once a week."

Milne soon got Emeli to write songs and accompany herself on the piano. "One of the things in theory that I do with most of my pupils is writing a tune to words, and that comes into the theory exams," he said. "Her songs became more complex and emotive and she began experimenting with different styles. She does a lot of composing now, and I hope that I may have helped set the ground stones for that."

If Milne had been in any doubt about the contribution he made towards Emeli's career, that disappeared when he opened the sleeve to her debut album, *Our Version Of Events.* "I noticed on her CD she said, 'I'd like to thank Ian Milne for showing me my way around the piano'. What I think she meant by that was that I showed her not just how to play a tune, but also how to get chords, because that helps you towards composing."

Milne, now 68, continues to teach music as a part-time music lecturer in teacher training at Aberdeen university and admits he has earned some kudos because of his association with Emeli. "It's funny when I look back on it," he admitted. "She just came to the house as a pupil and now she is a megastar ... some of [my] students have found out that I taught Emeli Sandé and that gives them some encouragement."

Eventually, those lessons would be enough to convince Emeli she could take to the stage to perform in front of a wider audience, and she had her sights on the Inverurie talent show. The contest, organised by the local Gordon District Council, was held in the town hall, a sort of 'Inverurie's Got Talent'.

So it was that when the day arrived, Joel packed up the gear and drove his daughter to the venue, both of them filled with nervous tension and excitement. Joel waited with trepidation for his daughter's turn to shine and then, staring out at the judges, her hair tied back in a ponytail, little Adele Emeli Sandé stepped onto the stage and belted out Liza Minnelli's 'Cabaret' and Mariah Carey's 'Never Forget You'.

Perhaps the first lesson the young singer learned during that early public performance was if at first you don't succeed, try, try again, because she failed to get through the audition stages at this first attempt. But she was not to be discouraged. Displaying a trait that would stand her in good stead when facing a string of rejections – some of them public – as an unknown trying to break into the music business, Emeli refused to give up and returned to take part in the Inverurie talent show on two subsequent occasions.

Her second attempt came the following year. Her choice of material proved that this was no ordinary wannabe; not for her the cheesy disco songs we hear from *X Factor* contestants or the latest one-hit wonder. If she was going to impress the judges, she would do it by singing the songs that had inspired her to make the trip in the first place.

Joel said: "She moved on to Christina Aguilera when she entered a second time and later chose the gospel song 'I Sing Because I'm Happy/His Eye Is On The Sparrow' and 'A Woman's Worth' by Alicia Keys.

This time she came a respectable third and collected a cheque for £150.

Ian Milne said: "The Inverurie talent show ran for quite a few years and she always added a great deal to the atmosphere because she was very different from the other contestants. It was a good start for her and a good grounding, because she was still at school."

A couple of years later Emeli returned to the show for a third time, this time as part of teenage a cappella trio Celeste. Milne believes Emeli exploited a loophole in the rules in order to take part on this third occasion: "I was the musical director that year and I arranged all the music," he said. "[Emeli] came back with Celeste because if you had been placed you couldn't enter again, so she came back as part of another act, which again shows how enthusiastic she was."

The plan worked. The young group of teenagers won first prize and celebrated with an even bigger prize pot of £500, split three ways between Emeli and her bandmates, Nadia Donald and Lorna Routh. Mum Diane, who has kept the piano on which Emeli wrote her earliest songs, said: "Winning with Celeste, when they sang 'Bridge Over Troubled Water' and 'Fields Of Gold' a cappella, was a fun night."

Despite Celeste's success, Emeli was intent on forging her own path: "I was part of a trio for a while. But the rest of the time I was just by myself. I guess in Alford there weren't too many people who liked the same kind of music as me, so I was flying solo."

It is with an immense amount of pride that the organisers of the Inverurie talent show can take some of the kudos for having not only encouraged, but also recognised the singer's talent. George Mitchell, who produced the show for the Gordon District Council, realised the event was blessed by Emeli's participation, not just in the years she placed first and third, but when she made her debut on the pop stage. "I have a distinct memory of sitting there on a cold Sunday morning at her very first audition," said George. "She came in, sang and everybody held their breath as they listened to her. She commanded the hall. We used to advise all the contestants on how they could improve their performance so we talked to Emeli, who was still known as Adele at that time. She listened and took on board everything we said. She was a lovely person in every sense of the word."

Cutbacks in music education led Morag Simpson to take voluntary redundancy from Alford Primary in 1997, but her reputation remains undiminished, Simpson having groomed Emeli for success from such a young age. She currently teaches up to 2,000 children each week as part of the Scottish government's Youth Music Initiative, and says Emeli's success is inspiring a whole new generation of young singers and musicians. "I have gone up in the estimation of the children in the schools I am teaching in now because I taught her," she said, laughing. "The kids think I am wonderful now. They are all sticking in with the choir. There were lots of musical kids when I taught Emeli, but she stood out as being talented enough to go on and do something with her music."

Simpson admits she is, however, slightly stunned by just how well Emeli has done since those ocarina and singing lessons in primary school. "I would never have guessed how far her talent would take her," she said. "I couldn't have predicted that. It is really amazing."

Long after fame came calling, Emeli made a point of returning to Alford Primary to celebrate with them in the run-up to Christmas 2012. "She told the pupils that, if they had a dream they should follow it," headteacher Liz MacLeod said. "She is a great role model for the children to have. She was so natural with [them] and there was great banter. I told her dad that if the singing didn't work out, she could become a teacher.

"During that visit, [she] reminded me that her very first solo performance was in our school Christmas production when she sang the lead part of Mary in *Hosanna Rock*. Even at such a young age she had a voice that was quite remarkable. Little did I know what great things were in store for her. I did, however, keep the programme for that nativity play, which was on the computer from 1997, and I was able to give her a copy. She was amazed I still had it – the graphics had gone because it was on an old computer, but she took it away with her. I must have known it would be worth keeping."

MacLeod added: "I don't think I will ever forget the look of surprise, shock and excitement on [the children's] happy faces. This was probably the hardest secret I have ever had to keep. I knew there was a chance [Emeli] would visit, but it was not confirmed until the Thursday before her arrival. None of the staff knew and so it was a total surprise for them too. It was such a lovely end to the term. Emeli spoke to the children and reminisced about sitting in assemblies in the same hall when she was a pupil in the school. She laughed at how it now looked so much smaller to her. She presented us with her framed award for selling a million copies of her album. This award is to be shared with the Academy and will be displayed in our joint dining hall. Emeli then asked if we would like her to sing. You can imagine the response to that. She sat down at the piano (which had been specially cleaned, dusted and polished – in secret – the night before) and sang her hit 'Next To Me' with all the children joining in the chorus, and 'Clown', which was to be her latest release. The children then had the opportunity to ask her lots of questions. What an early Christmas present for us all."

Considering the pupils had no time to prepare, their questions were excellent, leading to an exclusive that Emeli was learning to play the cello.

Emeli admits keeping her visit a secret had been the key to its success. "That was great. My mum had managed to organise the surprise with the headteacher from my primary school, and for the Academy as well. So we went and surprised the kids. It was their last day of term and they had just come back from their Christmas party and they weren't expecting it at all … It was a really lovely thing to do for Christmas, I think."

"She has been single-minded, but what is lovely is that she is still grounded and happy to come back and see her old primary school," MacLeod said. "We are all very proud."

Not half as proud as her parents, including dad, Joel, whom Emeli often singles out for praise. "My dad just loved female voices when I was a kid. Even though we were living in the middle of nowhere in Scotland he would tell me I should check out Nina Simone and Mariah Carey and Whitney and Anita Baker. It was just an amazing education … As I got older it was Joni Mitchell and Lauryn Hill.

All these women bring something very special to their music and I think I've been influenced by all of them. I felt very different and quite timid as a child and I'd find it very difficult to say things and express myself. So music became something where I could connect with people throughout the world. I could create my own platform and the way that I would have people listen to me – it became my expression really."

2. EMELI'S GOT TALENT

It has been widely reported that the first song Emeli wrote was called 'Tomorrow Starts Again' when she was just 11 years old, although sister, Lucy, recalls the pair of them writing together from an earlier age and being influenced by the music genres trending in the charts in the early nineties.

Emeli had written 'Tomorrow Starts Again' for her primary school talent show, the first of many she would take part in before leaving school. Apart from sounding like the name of a Bond movie, it's a great title for a song with a cleverness to it that seems at odds with the author's young age. Even at that time, Emeli was able to write a meaningful song with a solid structure. "It even had a middle eight," she said. "All my songs were about world peace and all these political issues. I had a lot of fun with all that."

It was also during this songwriting assignment that Emeli got her first lesson in plagiarism, when her classmates nicked most of her ideas. "I thought, well, if it's worth stealing then it might be all right," Emeli said. "That was the first time I thought I might be a songwriter. I always knew I wanted to be a musician, and I always knew I wanted to write, because the people I was listening to all wrote. I never thought it was an option to sing anyone else's songs."

Being one of her earliest attempts, the song was also a chance for Emeli to develop the skill long before she would be tested by professionals in the music business, and considered both as a songwriter for hire and as a singer in her own right. While there is an army of young hopefuls queueing up each year to take part in *The X Factor*, each of them desperate to try their hand at classic pop tunes, that was never going to be enough for Emeli. When she wrote 'Tomorrow Starts Again' she believed she had found her calling, and she began making serious plans to make her dream come true.

By the time Emeli hit her teens she was performing more widely around Aberdeenshire. One such performance drew the attention of professional footballer David Craig who would go on to help her develop her career. Craig spotted the 13-year-old singing in Aberdeen's city centre while standing atop a float during a parade. The girl with the dark-auburn afro was taking part in an Afro-Caribbean festival and her vocal talent and song choice was remarkable enough to make him put down his shopping bags and watch. David, at that point a footballer for Aberdeen FC and later a player for lower league clubs and then in the Spanish and Hong Kong leagues, recognised her talent, but he had no idea back then he would play a part in helping the girl on the festival float to stardom.

"I just thought there was something special about her then. There was a parade going through Union Street. I think [she did] a Roberta Flack cover, 'Killing Me Softly'. Firstly, I was surprised and thought it strange that someone so young would know about Roberta Flack. I was also struck by how good her voice was ... It was the last thing you expected to hear walking down Aberdeen's town centre on a Saturday afternoon. There was something a little bit different about her. You could tell she had talent ... I don't know if even at that point she had any ambitions to be a singer or if it was just something she did and she was good at. Certainly, I thought there was something special about her, but I didn't give it much thought until about three or four years later when our paths crossed again."

In the meantime, Emeli continued her piano lessons and developed her songwriting. By the time she had reached her mid-teens, she was gaining a profile beyond the confines of her local area. In July 2001, at just 15, she travelled to Croydon to make the first London appearance of her career, billed under her birth name Adele Sandé. Via its Rapology night in a local club, Choice FM was running a competition that aimed to seek out the best young unsigned singers and rappers in the UK. It had received over 3,000 demo CDs and whittled them down to 24 finalists. Emeli made the shortlist. The lucky winner would get the chance to record a demo single with Sony Records, £500 cash, Sony hardware and a trophy. But although presenter Richard Blackwood was impressed with the young Scottish girl with the big voice, it wasn't to be. Some years later, Blackwood would reflect on the meeting: "The weirdest thing is, I saw her perform, but it was so many years ago that I didn't realise the girl I saw and Emeli were the same person," he said. "Obviously everybody has heard of her now, but at the time I just thought she was a girl called Adele who had a lot of talent. I saw that she was at the VMAs in America last year, and it's so weird because years ago I said she was a star in the making and look at her now. She's gone through the roof. I wish I could lie, but I didn't know it was the girl from all those years ago I didn't know it was her. I only vaguely remember meeting her."

He does recall heading to Croydon that night without any great expectation of finding a new star to light up the music world. "Rapology was basically a place to discover new talent. People would come up and do their thing," Blackwood explained. "It didn't necessarily catapult you onto the mainstream if you did well on it. It was an underground scene ... it was informal. If you had any talent, you would go on there. The underground would talk about you and you would get your name out. It is evident now with [Emeli's] career how she got on there."

Blackwood became the first, but not the last, DJ and presenter to be confused by the singer, who at that time was still known as Adele and would change her name not once but twice in an effort to carve out an identity for herself. "I had to be reminded that I had bigged up Emeli Sandé when she [broke through]," Blackwood said. "I was like, how do I know that girl? I was working with so many artists at MTV every day. You see some people with raw talent but don't know if they will follow it through."

Someone else who had begun to realise Emeli was something special at that time was another urban DJ and BBC presenter, Trevor Nelson, who gave Sandé one of her first big breaks when she took part in yet another talent contest. Lucy Sandé had filmed her sister at the piano singing the song 'Nasty Little Lady' and entered the video into Nelson's BBC Urban Music competition.

"I had a TV show called *The Lowdown* on the BBC and my producers were keen that there was an aspect of it that discovered new talent," Nelson said. "Reggie Yates hosted that part of the show for me and you had to watch the show to know about it because it was pretty much under the radar. I'd be lying if I told you I remembered it all. I did remember a girl called Adele... she was called Adele Sandé at the time. What struck me was it was just a girl on the keyboards, sitting down Alicia Keys-style, singing a song I think she wrote."

This time, Emeli won the top prize: a record deal with a now defunct record label, Telstar. However, despite being just 16, she decided to reject the offer. Father, Joel, said: "She had a record deal on the table, but she got the chance to go to university. She had to turn [the deal] down. Having read through the contract, it didn't give her enough security or longevity. It was just for one single and maybe one other after that. She needed something to fall back on."

Joel believes his daughter's choice between furthering her education or concentrating on a music career was a tough one, and he admits that he did his best to persuade his daughter to put her studies first, out of concern that the music business, notorious for eating up and spitting out young talent, might leave her high and dry.

"She had decided to take a year out to concentrate on music when she left Alford Academy after sixth year," he said. "That was a time when the record companies didn't know what to do with her. They called her down to London for showcases, but time was running out. She had to make her mind up whether or not to go to university. She finally made the decision to carry on with her chosen career of medicine. We thought her music career would be sorted out during that year out, but it never happened. That was another hurdle. Inherently, she must have been thinking that things were happening that would eventually get her to the top. When things weren't working out for her or she didn't make it, we were there to say that something is going to happen, because look at the people at the top. People like Beyoncé or Mariah Carey. I would tell her, these guys started just like you started. They live in a different part of the world, but you are professional like them."

Emeli also sensed that turning down the deal with Telstar was the right move. "Doing the rounds of labels, I just didn't like it. I just thought, I'd rather be a bit more in control than this," she said. "It was hard at the time because it was so tempting, but I was doing my exams at school, then I got accepted into medicine at Glasgow uni. It would have been too much of a risk to say no to medicine, then go down to London and be just another singer."

The teenage singer returned to Scotland empty handed, unaware that Carlton Dixon, a producer for BBC3, had spotted her talent and tipped off music business acquaintance Adrian Sykes.

Sykes, who is now Emeli's manager and trusted friend, recalls: "Carlton told me he had found a great girl and that I had to go and see her. Being London-centric, I thought he was going to send me south of the Thames. When he told me she was actually in Aberdeen, I was like, 'Oh, God, really?' But he persuaded me to go. Danny D, a music publisher friend of mine, and I got on a plane, got a taxi from the airport to her house, met the family and sat down to this lovely little girl plinking out some tunes. She performed a song called 'Matchstick Girl'. Even at 16, she was clearly incredibly talented. She was still at school, a grade-A student, just about to take her Highers. She had a great determination and she was writing really good songs even then. She was just about to blossom."

Mum, Diane, said: "Adrian came up to the house after the *Lowdown* competition. We have known him for a long time. He was right behind her when she started her medicine degree. No matter how much faith you have in your child the music industry is so difficult. People say things are going to happen and then things change. The fact that she chose to go and do her degree showed a lot of maturity. She didn't place all her eggs in one basket. She was sensible enough to get her university degree and decided it would be important and valuable. Of course, she gets all her brains, beauty and talent from her mum!"

Understandably mistrustful of the music business, Emeli's dad, Joel, taped the conversation as Sykes pitched for a chance to develop her career. "People came and schmoozed and talked about the good things and never about the downside of the industry," Joel said. "I wanted to make sure we could review what had been said before making any decisions. So I recorded all the meetings of the people who came over."

"I can understand why he felt the need to tape those conversations," Sykes said. "We were the big record company people coming up from London. Joel and Diane were brilliant with us though, incredibly courteous and welcoming. They were genuinely pleased that someone else believed in their daughter the way they did."

Despite what could have been seen as another setback to her career, Emeli remained positive thanks to the backing of her family and Sykes' support. He would keep a watchful eye on Emeli as she developed her music while she studied medicine at the University of Glasgow for the next four years.

"I always had the utmost faith in Emeli, even during the ups and downs," her sister, Lucy, said. "When Emeli was 16, when she met Trevor Nelson, things didn't go to plan. But I always knew that she would keep going and eventually everything would happen for her, that one day everyone would hear her music. Even all through university, she kept on singing."

"I think... I was just 17 and I wanted to get, you know, away from my parents a little bit, but not too far away so I could still take washing home," Emeli said of her choice to put her education first. "I didn't want to move too far away but I still wanted to feel independent."

The University of Glasgow, founded in 1451, is the fourth oldest English-speaking university in the world; alumni include engineer James Watt; John Logie Baird, inventor of the world's first television; economist Adam Smith; seven Nobel laureates and two British prime ministers, Bonar Law and Sir Henry Campbell-Bannerman. Steeped in history, with a mix of ancient and modern architecture, the university was an inspirational place for Emeli to study to become a doctor, but there were constant reminders of her other dream, since the university's Queen Margaret Union, which often doubled as a concert hall, was just a stone's throw away. Queen, Motörhead, Red Hot Chili Peppers and Nirvana have all played there in years past, packing in 900 students a time. The nearby University Union also put on occasional gigs, including Arcade Fire, Bombay Bicycle Club and comedian Jerry Sadowitz.

Although Emeli had her degree to think about, she still wanted her music to be heard. She admits she was stretched to breaking point during those years as she attempted to pass her exams and land a record deal at the same time. "It was difficult, and the further I got on in the course it became more so because I was falling asleep in lectures, and at the shows I was thinking about medicine, so it got quite difficult. I was still making a lot of music. To me, I just really wanted to have a degree, to properly finish school. It was always something my dad said was very important so I wanted to study and the whole challenge of medicine really excited me. Sometimes I did think maybe I'll be a doctor, but I kind of knew I'm only going to be really happy if I become a musician."

As Emeli dreamed of music stardom, she got involved with like-minded musicians and budding music execs in Glasgow and further afield, all the time being sure to work hard at university. "I was a big geek. I took the hardest classes I could, all the sciences. I loved being at the top."

She had to pick a specialised field and her fascination with the brain, which she describes as being "like a black hole", convinced her that neuroscience would be a perfect fit. "It's vast and fascinating. I'm fascinated by psychiatry and mental breakdown."

Her studies meant she had to face the realities of her prospective career early on. "In Glasgow university [in medicine] you come into contact with dead human bodies in first year," she said. "It's kind of like, this is what you're going to be doing for the next five years so you'd better get used to it. In the actual uni there is an anatomy section and you go down a big tunnel and it's there. Thankfully people are still donating their bodies to medical research, for med students to explore. And it's interesting because you feel so removed from the fact that these were once actual people… it was a bizarre experience. I was learning from a dead body and I think the thing that brought it home to me was when we were looking at the brain, because we would be using a real brain which would be passed round, but there was nothing there. Inside that brain there used to be dreams, ideas and thoughts, but now it was just organic. Just a piece of flesh. So that really made me think. Where did they go? Where is that person?"

If for any reason her music career suddenly crumbled, Emeli insists she would dust herself off and get back to her other love. "It would take me a while to get over it and then I would re-apply to go back to university, and I would train to be either a psychiatrist or a neurologist," she said. "That would be the plan."

While Emeli excelled in her studies, she was also quickly accepted into the thriving local music scene. She started playing piano and singing jazz standards in the city's hotels in order to help fund her studies and express herself into the bargain. These low-key gigs, the type that are often ignored by hotel patrons coming and going from business meetings, gave Emeli a chance to relax away from the gruelling university coursework. It was also a chance to develop her songwriting, although the pressure of exams made it difficult to stick with her craft. If there was a point when Emeli could have crashed and burned and left her music career aspirations in the dust, this would be it. The high intensity of her studies began to take a toll and her creativity faltered.

"I had a lot of writer's block and my head was full of facts and exams. I found it really hard to experience anything to write about other than sitting in the library," Emeli said. "But I was doing shows and everyone on the course knew I was a musician. My writing speeded up, though, as soon as I started going down to London and meeting producers there. Before, it was just me and a piano so the sounds I could make were quite limited."

This from the girl who would soon lay down demos for songs such as 'Kill The Boy', with the explosive opening lyric 'I walk around with a bullet on my tongue/Killer written on my face', and 'Daddy', which deals with addiction. "Any time I write something that's trying to be too smart, it doesn't work. 'Kill The Boy' was the first idea that came into my head. Any song I have to work on longer than a day, I just leave it. It's not gonna work. Everything that's good is really instant," she revealed of her songwriting style.

Later, the stripped-down demos would become string-drenched recordings. It was just that Emeli had yet to realise her potential.

3. URBAN SCOT

It was while studying at university that Emeli met three young Scots who helped transform her from a wallflower into a confident and accomplished entertainer. David Craig, who had left football for a career in DJing and promotion, was among the trio. He and his colleagues, Mel Awasi and Laura McCrum, had teamed up to run Urban Scot, an organisation to promote up-and-coming music of black origin in Scotland. Urban Scot's existence was a godsend to musicians who didn't fit into the predominantly white indie scene and who wanted to create soul, jazz, hip hop, R&B, fusion and rap, all genres of music that had been under-represented for so long in Scotland.

Laura McCrum said: "David, Mel and I set up Urban Scot in 2005 … This wasn't about finding black artists. There were a lot of artists involved in music of black origin in Scotland, but they weren't getting airplay down in London or further afield. We wanted to start doing nights where we could book a bigger-name act and get the local support artists to warm up for them and get industry professionals to come along and see the talent we have here in Scotland. Emeli was one of the people who answered our call for artists in 2005."

Awasi recalls: "We never signed an artist, nor would we claim that anybody was ours. A lot of people wanted to be managed by us but it was more about doing short classes and seminars for a group of people. We used to scout artists around Scotland. We had a number of regular showcase events and we organised the concerts and we did a couple of small festivals. With a showcase event the aim was to provide a platform for urban Scottish artists. But that was quite limited ... the urban scene in Scotland wasn't as big as it is now. The turn-out would be 50 to 100 bodies. Some artists were performing for the very first time, but it wasn't giving them the exposure we wanted. So we decided to bring some national and international artists as headliners and Scottish artists would get the opportunity to perform with them. Dave had found out about Emeli in Aberdeen and we got involved."

Craig recalls: "Anytime we had showcases on around the country where we were booking the headliners we would get [Emeli] to be one of the warm-up acts. Those gigs were usually in Glasgow, Edinburgh or Aberdeen. The only reason I figured out that it was the same girl I had seen on the float years before was because somebody told me she was a young kid from Alford. Later, through chatting to her, I figured out that it was her."

McCrum recalls her first meeting with the girl who would go on to mesmerise the nation, but who gave little indication of her ability to turn heads at the bus stop, let alone a global audience of over a billion at the London 2012 Summer Olympic Games Opening Ceremony. Rather, McCrum remembers a shy and introverted teenager who was a million miles away from the confident wannabes she was used to seeing on the urban circuit in Scotland. "She was timid and quite a reserved young lady," she said. "I've got to be honest, when I first spoke to her I couldn't believe she wanted to be a singer. Most of the singers you meet are quite full of themselves and quite bolshy."

However, her impression of Emeli changed when she heard her soundcheck at her first Urban Scot concert at the Aberdeen Lemon Tree. "Notoriously, whenever you do a gig and want to soundcheck your artists it can be an absolute nightmare to get them in," she said.

"You want to soundcheck them before the punters come into the venue, but a lot of performers feel they shouldn't have to turn up hours before they are due to go onstage. Emeli was never like that. She was very sweet and a very quiet little girl who was always on time.

"I'll never ever forget the first time I heard her sing. She came into the Lemon Tree for her soundcheck. There were a few cleaners, a guy was sweeping the floor. But everybody in the place just stopped what they were doing. Literally, the guy with the broom nearly dropped it. It was one of those moments. Everybody was like, what a voice on this tiny girl who was 17 years old. She was so polite and quiet and meek, then she opened her mouth to sing and we were all blown away. I was like, oh my goodness.

"When you put out a call for artists people send in their CDs and sometimes, when it is a homemade CD or something made in the bedroom, you can't get a good grasp of what the voice is like and what the performance is going to be like. The recording she sent was fine, but it was night and day from her soundchecking in the venue even before going on to perform live. As soon as I heard her sing I thought this girl has got what it takes."

Awasi added: "The first time I saw Emeli was at the gig that night. I told Dave she was amazing. We couldn't believe she was from Aberdeen. One of the songs had a sampling of Nina Simone's [version of the gospel track] 'Nobody's Fault But Mine'. I grew up listening to Motown and soul, so when she did her part in the song I just couldn't believe it. I remember standing there thinking, this sounds like Nina Simone. The power of her voice was my first exposure to Adele, or Emeli as she's known now. I saw the rawness."

Awasi also agrees with McCrum's assessment of Emeli having been a young and timid girl yet to find her own voice offstage. "She was definitely a shy girl," he said. "I remember her being quite shy and quite reserved as well. There are other artists we've worked with who are more out there. She didn't say much. She was a nice person. She had finished school and this was at the start of her university studies and compared to the other artists we worked with she was very different to them all. The rest were more in your face and more actively trying to make that break. Her shyness gave her a more laid-back attitude. That and the fact that her focus at the time was on completing her degree."

McCrum, who felt an immediate affinity with the teenager from Alford, said: "In the early days, you could tell she was quite nervous, but as soon as she played the first few chords on the piano and started to sing, it would go away. I can't say I knew she would make it and be big and famous but personally I had such a strong feeling towards her. We are both mixed race, we were both brought up in Scotland and we both had the same hair. When she came in I felt she was like a little sister. Certainly from the moment I saw her I wanted her to do well. A voice like that is a God-given talent. A lot of people out there want to be singers and dancers. They're OK but don't have the vocals to do it, but Emeli was something special."

By the summer of 2007, Laura McCrum had been given her own show on BBC Radio Scotland, called *Blackstreet*. She began Emeli's media training in preparation for her first ever radio spot.

"We didn't see each other on a day-to-day basis, but I got my own show at the BBC and she was the first guest I wanted to get into the Live Lounge," McCrum said. "Getting her in to play live was wonderful. I'm told that was the first UK play of her music. The timing was really good because Urban Scot was at its height. It helped Adele, as she was known then, and other artists get airplay and recognition. It wouldn't have been the first episode, which was pre-recorded. It was the second episode of 2007 in the summer of that year. She came on and had a chat and sang some songs. When she came in, it was her first time in a studio and her first time as a featured artist being interviewed. She sang in one of the studios with a sound engineer pre-recording and we played that on air as live."

It's hard to believe the million-selling chart star Emeli Sandé, who now guests on television shows several times a week, was a bit of a stammering wreck in her early interviews. However, a simple tip helped her to overcome her awkwardness. "She was really nervous and excited before we went on air that first time," McCrum said. "I do remember telling her that if she felt nervous at any point to smile because if she smiled it would change the tone of her voice and she wouldn't sound nervous. She beamed throughout the whole interview. It was lovely."

The media training continued and Emeli's uncomplicated nature and willingness to concentrate on the positive rather than the negative aspects of the local music scene gave her an edge over contemporaries.

"We offered her, as well as the other artists, media training. It was good practice for a young artist," McCrum reveals. "Especially for the boys; they want to be hip hop stars and rappers. They might be talented, but some had a real resentment because they felt they were being overlooked by the rest of the UK. The MOBO Awards were very fresh at the time, for example, and had yet to come into their own. The work we did with them was more to deal with the fact that they came in with resentment and to explain that this would be what they got back.

"Adele never had a chip on her shoulder but she needed to speak up for herself a little bit more. She needed confidence-building exercises. I think of someone like Jessie J, who is loud and bolshy and in your face. She is a good example because Jessie J won the BRITs Critics' Choice award the year before Emeli did. I remember they were both being interviewed together on a TV show just after Emeli had won the award. Jessie J was all bolshy and Emeli was quiet and nice and polite. She was dwarfed by Jessie. Sometimes when you are in that field, you need to keep that focus on you because that could be your 15 minutes. It is brilliant that it hasn't played against her and she has managed to be herself, but when she started out she would get onstage and sing her songs and there would be no audience interaction. The work we did at Urban Scot helped her with stage presence. You want a bit of banter with the audience if someone is restringing a guitar or if something goes wrong so that you don't lose your audience, and Urban Scot helped with that."

Despite forming a bond, the pair couldn't hang out as much as they might have liked. "It's sad to say we didn't get to spend a lot of time together because I was based in Edinburgh and she was in Aberdeen but we did have a good relationship," McCrum said. "Every time I saw her there was a big smile and a big hug and such warmth. I'm a single parent and my daughter would come to some of the performances. She was always interested in what my daughter was doing and would play with her in the green room."

Of her first interview on *Blackstreet*, Awasi said: "...the feedback was unbelievable with people phoning in. She had a demo CD but she was still quite young and hadn't had a lot of exposure and limited experience in performing. We came in at the start and I'm not saying we helped. We were just a tool that gave her an opportunity."

The team had also set up a website with an online magazine and a directory of urban artists and related businesses based in Scotland, which enabled Emeli and the other up-and-coming artists to build relationships with other musicians and contacts. "We had an artist directory that had singers, producers and people with studio space all on there. It became a forum. People would meet at gigs and start working together. We knew that Adele was making links with other people and that was fully supported," Awasi said. "We were there in the early stages of her career and we did artist mentoring. We featured her extensively on our website. She did a couple of gigs in Aberdeen in the Karma Lounge and we asked her to support some of the international artists. I remember speaking to her; she was very focused on what she wanted to do and what she wanted to do at the time was her medical degree. Everything was secondary to that."

While it is amazing to think that Emeli might have become a doctor at the expense of a career in pop music, Awasi believes she made the right decision to carry on her studies until she completed her degree. "If her father knew the potential but also what she could have been, maybe he would have pushed her to get more involved," he said. "It is hard to tell if her father influenced her or if it was her desire to put her degree first before getting involved in the industry."

Cynics might suggest Emeli saw an opportunity to perform in front of a receptive audience when in 2007 she participated in an event organised by Pan African Arts Scotland to celebrate the bicentennial anniversary celebrations of the passing into law of the Slavery Abolition Act 1833, but it was simply her social conscience that drove her there.

The event took place at Glasgow's Old Fruitmarket venue. A functioning market from the Victorian period until the seventies, the Old Fruitmarket is now a stunning concert hall with a high vaulted ceiling and space for 1,200 people across two levels consisting of the huge courtyard and balcony. Emeli would return to the venue as part of a UK tour after enjoying the sort of chart success she could only dream of back in 2007. As part of the bicentennial celebration, Pan African Arts Scotland's CEO and Artistic Director, Gameli Tordzro, also recorded a music video: "We had a project called the Freedom Project, which included a music video that I directed and that involved a number of budding musicians at the time. She was one of them; she did 'Change Has Come' and a number of other songs."

Tordzro was so impressed with Emeli that he offered to put the recordings on YouTube, in order for her music to reach a wider audience.

"Once we worked with [Emeli] in 2007, I offered to do a number of things for her which would promote her talent," Tordzro said. "I recorded some of her performances... Both shows that she performed for us were at the Old Fruitmarket venue and we still have the music video we made and distributed, but we haven't publicised it. One of the reasons is that when she became popular, she asked that we take down the video we had done of her on YouTube. I still have those videos on my YouTube channel but that is not public. The Freedom DVD was published, but we haven't pursued pushing it at all. When I say it was published, we never sold them. We just distributed them to people who came to our show and interested parties. We pressed up 200 copies, so it wasn't a massive product."

Describing those early performances by Emeli, Tordzro admits he was blown away, echoing the words of so many others who could not believe the talented singer was an unknown struggling to generate interest in her songs.

"The exciting thing was I saw a highly talented young woman," he said. "One of our main aims is to create opportunities and also encourage people who have talent to shine, and that's what we set out to do. One of the first things I told her was that she was world class and that she had to believe in herself, and I think that's what she did, but at the time Emeli just smiled. I have a feeling that she was like so many young people of African heritage in Scotland who are incredibly talented and don't even know just how talented they are."

Even if Emeli was something of a wallflower during her early encounters with the music industry in Scotland, pretty soon she had a very clear idea of her talent, as she explained to Urban Scot's David Craig when she confided she had "built a vocal foundation by listening to the great divas, for example Mariah and Aretha" to strengthen her voice.

"As I grew older I began listening to more subtle artists such as Nina Simone, D'Angelo and Miles Davis," she told him. "These artists made me look deeper into my lyrics and musicianship. A lot of literature has also influenced my music. I think it's important to take inspiration from as many different areas of life as possible."

Craig said: "I don't want to say that before that she was shy. Shy probably isn't the right word, but she would just get up onstage and sing her songs and then disappear without saying too much. She would make a massive impression onstage and then disappear back into herself as soon as she was finished. It was simply all about the music for her. She would come on and she would play and wouldn't hang out and socialise that much. She would just sit there quietly and take things in.

"As the years went by and the more gigs she did, she just seemed more comfortable being up there in front of a crowd to the point where, later on and coming towards the end of the Urban Scot stuff and coming towards the end of her time at uni, the confidence really grew and she looked like an artist. It came together naturally for her. The more she played the more confidence she got, to the point where she was believable as a star.

"The best thing we did for her was to give her a stage to perform on and an audience to sing in front of really. We can't take more credit than that. As little as that sounds, it's a big thing. As an artist you need to be singing live in front of a crowd. Starting out, it isn't easy for a new artist to get gigs. I remember her in one gig telling people to be quiet in the nicest possible way. When you are starting out people can be chatting at gigs and the acts before the headline act often don't get the respect. As she developed, she wasn't shy about telling people that she wanted their attention."

David Craig and the Urban Scot team were determined to get Emeli seen by the biggest of industry names via the headline acts they promoted at their showcases. "It was whoever was on the scene touring at that moment," Craig said. "Most of the shows covered the costs or ran at a loss, but the idea was to provide a platform for these guys coming through. I think it helped a lot of them. You could clearly see they were improving, Emeli particularly. There was a three- or four-year period just doing gigs and seeing her socially and I was able to watch her progress and grow as an artist."

Meanwhile, the relationship with Urban Scot enabled Emeli to get her early recordings to a wider audience. "We'd put together a mix CD of the artists who performed at the lounge to give people who didn't attend an opportunity to listen to the artists," Awasi said. "We would record the show or ask the artist to give us the tracks they were recording. We would do that with most of the showcases we hosted. In Emeli's case we did both. We had live tracks and demo tracks. We would burn the tracks and distribute them freely, either at the gig or after the gig. We couldn't compare the feedback we had with Emeli to any of the other artists on those CDs. People would tell us she was amazing and that they wanted to hear more of her stuff. I still have the recordings somewhere. They are in a box, in the cellar at my dad's house in Glasgow where my stuff from back home is stored."

By this point, it wasn't just Scotland that was getting its first taste of the Afro-haired singer. As November 2008 approached, she prepared for a performance at the Independent Music Show, held at the Bullet Bar in north-west London. In an interview with presenter Helen Shephard before the show, she admitted she was already hopeful of a career in the music business.

She explained: "I feel that my music is very fresh for the UK. I don't feel there is anybody doing something so raw with their voice. I really love the music scene right now in the UK, but I really feel there is a market for something quite raw, quite soulful, just really honest."

Among the songs she performed that night, accompanied on a Roland keyboard, was 'Baby's Eyes'. Belting out the ballad, she revealed her incredible and big, soulful voice. If it sounded as though the song meant something personal, it was because the song was about Emeli's first serious boyfriend.

"When I started writing songs, when I was about 13, I promised myself I would never write a love song because that's what everyone else does," she told Shephard. "But I got to about 16 or 17 and I found a boy, so that was my first ever love song. I'm really glad I didn't write it in a cheesy manner because it still means the same to me now."

Meanwhile, Emeli became the main act at the nights that David Craig set up in Aberdeen to showcase local talent. "The gigs that I did up in Aberdeen called the Karma Lounge were for unsigned acts from around the country," Craig said. "I think Emeli was probably 17 or 18 by then, I would imagine. A couple of nights stood out.

One at the Lemon Tree in Aberdeen. I opened that night as a DJ. She had got a bit of a shine as a songwriter, but not as a singer. I hadn't seen her in a year and a half and that was when I realised she was a star in the making."

As well as hearing newly penned songs that would eventually make their way onto her debut album, *Our Version Of Events*, and into the homes of the listening public, Craig got a preview of songs yet to be released. One of those was an early love song written for long-term boyfriend Adam Gouraguine. "She used to perform a couple of songs regularly that didn't make the album, including one that she wrote for Adam, which was fantastic," he said. "I don't know if they will ever see the light of day. I have a couple of those early demos that never made the album, but most of the songs that are on the album were written after that."

As usual, Emeli's parents were front and centre, making sure their daughter was in safe hands. Joel busied himself at the shows by keeping a video record of her performances, some of which have since been posted to YouTube and reveal the fledgling artist enjoying and experimenting with her sound.

"Her dad recorded absolutely everything," Craig said. "Joel and Diane never missed a gig, whether it was a Tuesday night in Edinburgh or a Friday night in Glasgow. They were always there so there will be a wealth of video footage of Emeli in those early years. The Karma Lounge was monthly for a little while and we did Urban Scot live shows. She would be involved in them in one way or another performing."

Among the songs Emeli performed at the Karma Lounge in Aberdeen's Lemon Tree venue in early 2009 was 'Booty Call', a track that has a riff similar to Daft Punk's 'Get Lucky', yet this song, too, was one of many in her repertoire that never made it onto her debut album. The performance does, however, appear on YouTube. With Emeli wearing a checked shirt and this time backed by a full band, the funk-laden performance shows that she was experimenting with her usual old-school soul/gospel music style.

However, although Emeli was gaining confidence and pushing her music into new territory, headliner status still eluded her. During a Karma Lounge concert, this time held at the Tunnels nightclub in Aberdeen, she took second billing to another female soul singer, L-Marie. But it wasn't long before she made top billing. On January 24, 2009, Emeli again played the Karma Lounge, but this time as the headline act, with Ghanaian rapper Kobi Onyame and Edinburgh-based hip hop act Young Fathers in support. Promotion for the event boasted "the very best in unsigned and home-grown musicians and performers."

In fact, by now, Emeli had become Urban Scot's principal protégé. As part of this privilege, she enjoyed valuable experience performing as a support act to bigger names, such as Los Angeles hip hop act the Pharcyde. One gig in particular almost provided Emeli with an opportunity to break through. Urban Scot had booked MC Guru (who had made his name as a member of hip hop duo Gang Starr) to play an Edinburgh show in the shadow of the Royal Mile, famously populated by tourists and packed during the Edinburgh festival. Emeli was booked as support, giving her the opportunity to perform in front of Guru and his team, as well as his fans. And Guru wasn't disappointed, to the point he wanted to collaborate with Emeli when he next returned to the UK.

"We thought Emeli would be ideal for a project with Guru," Craig said. "The collaboration was talked about and his label loved her. They thought she was fantastic and she made a great impression. She would have been ideal for that kind of project. They really liked her."

Sadly, it wasn't to be. The American rapper, producer and dancer – named by About.com as one of the Top 50 MCs of our time and ranked by Source as one of the Top 30 lyricists of all time – fell ill soon after the concert in Scotland. He was just 48 when he died from cancer in April 2010. "It was only ever talked about, so I can't say for sure that it would have happened, but they loved her and she made a massive impression."

Sadly for the Urban Scot team, there was more bad news to come in the form of a concert they staged for American hip hop and R&B star Akon. The multi-Grammy nominated rapper found fame in 2004 with the 'street single' 'Locked Up', which was followed by his first worldwide hit, 'Lonely', both of which appeared on his debut album, *Trouble*. He had gone on to have massive success worldwide, so Urban Scot expected a sell-out for the July 2007 show at the Braehead Arena, near Glasgow. However, the appetite for the gig wasn't as strong as they might have hoped, and the company found itself heavily in debt. It was to spell the beginning of the end for Urban Scot.

"[The company] was funded through personal funds. It was us putting money in," Awasi said. "It was difficult to get the business model right and it was hard for us to compete with big promoters … When we put Akon on at Braehead Arena, we thought we would at least break even or make a little money we could invest. We had plans to start a little festival on the back of that concert because the projected figures were good, but we didn't sell enough tickets and ended up losing a lot of money. It was hard to maintain the momentum afterwards. I started to back away from it and concentrate more on my engineering career. It was hard for us as an organisation to keep going."

Emeli hadn't attended the show, despite being on the bill as a support act. "We put her on the bill but then she pulled out because she had exams at the time or some other commitment," Awasi said. It wasn't a surprise to Awasi – he had become aware of the firm grip that Joel had on his daughter's future and his determination not to let her be sweet-talked into anything foolish.

"The last time I met her dad was at that festival we organised at Kelvingrove Park," he said. "Unfortunately, it rained the day of the festival and it wasn't a great turnout, but I said to her dad that she was amazing and world class and that he maybe needed to release her a bit. He said, 'Let her do her degree then she can do what she wants'. He was looking out for her. She could have gone into the music industry at an earlier age but there is no guarantee. There was no crystal ball you could look into that guaranteed that she'd be a big star. Her dad wanted something for her to fall back on. Obviously she is very talented and a lot of fathers with a son or daughter who can sing would think they are amazing, but he was being more realistic. It maybe gave Emeli a chance to mature a little bit before she got fully involved. You can hear it in her music, which is not as poppy as a lot of the stuff out there, which is too commercialised. She is different to a lot of the sounds that are coming out and so she is selling. People love her. It doesn't matter where you are, whether you are in Scotland, the rest of the UK or where I am out here in Qatar, people love her. Her father probably just wanted to make sure that she had a plan B to fall back on, and that's why he pushed her to concentrate on uni first."

David Craig also believes the Sandés' realistic outlook on life is what makes Emeli different. "Obviously, things blew up for her after she finished her studies," he said. "It's been nice sitting back and seeing how well she has been doing. Actually, it's great to see that an artist like her can progress and be successful. She's somebody who is the opposite of what you would expect from a pop artist these days. For me, she has always been pretty unique in the sense that she has never really made any effort to conform to what is in the charts. She has always been pretty headstrong about writing and in the way she writes and being herself. She seems to have succeeded in spite of that.

"I remember asking her how a young girl could write about things that touched me or things she had never experienced. I couldn't understand how she could be so mature as a writer when she maybe hadn't been through the things she was writing about. The other artists were also unsigned and a few of them are still around. The majority have just reverted back to day jobs and aren't working in a professional capacity. A couple are doing all right but none of them made the progression that Emeli did."

Though Craig, Mel Awasi and Laura McCrum had to give up Urban Scot after the unfortunate Akon concert, Emeli's success is far more satisfying than any profits they might have accrued. The team had championed the festival float girl, and she had already come a long way since that fortuitous day when David Craig happened upon the rising star. Even so, Craig insists her success is all her own doing. "I don't think we can take any credit for her being as great as she is. It was coincidental that we were there to help with bits and pieces," he says. "Everything is down to her and her talent. I don't think we did anything other than give her a platform to showcase how talented she is.

"The beautiful thing for me is that she never ever showed any interest in being famous. That's what I love about her. She only did it for the music. She loved the music and she is passionate about what she does. But the end result for her was never about being famous. There were all sorts of deals on the table from different labels. She had offers before she left school. She was always headstrong about going to school, getting that part done, getting the education sorted and then seeing what happened naturally afterwards. After the Trevor Nelson thing, there was big interest in her. She was never in a hurry. She never seemed to feel pressure to do it other than on her own terms. Anytime I spoke to her, I loved that she wanted to sing and write about things that mattered. She just wanted to be the artist she is. That's why I'm so surprised that she made it so big as a pop star.

"The good thing about when she did get a deal is that her label, Virgin EMI, as far as I can see, never pushed her. They never forced her into anything. They nurtured her as a songwriter first, they put time and effort into her and they allowed her to evolve as such. When the time was right they did it properly. You don't see that much these days with labels and artists and you don't see many people like Emeli, who is totally unaffected by what she has achieved and everything that she is."

Craig, who now works in Dubai, got the chance to see how Emeli's talent was beginning to attract a wider international audience.

"She came out here to Dubai to perform just before she got signed," he said. "It was nice to see – I don't want to say a shy little girl – but after all those years it was nice to see the end result of her as an artist, as Emeli Sandé. At the Dubai gig people were chatting and she told them, 'You've paid to come and see me so I would appreciate it if you would stop talking.' We have a festival here in Dubai called Sandance – I am resident DJ – and we can't afford her. I laugh about that now. That's a funny thing. We had her in a little room. I don't want to be clichéd and say you won't meet a nicer person, but she is just a fantastic person who is great at what she does. She has no arrogance about her whatsoever, despite how popular she has become now."

Mel Awasi, who left Scotland in 2009 to go to Thailand before working as an engineer in Qatar, added: "I kept in contact every now and then with the guys back in Scotland. I remember walking around one of the shopping malls in Bangkok and she was on the radio. I couldn't believe it. When I left she was just starting to work with [songwriter and record producer] Naughty Boy in London. Before she released her first single, 'Diamonds', somebody sent it to me. I remember listening to it and that was the song on the radio as I was wandering around the supermarket in Bangkok. I was so pleased she had made it. She is a nice girl who was different from others. She wasn't up herself. I don't know what she is like now but I bet she hasn't changed. I've met some very successful musicians who are very down to earth and I can imagine her being like that. I'm really pleased at how she has done and I hope we get the chance to see her in the Middle East and Qatar."

Laura McCrum shares the feelings of her former colleagues. "There was a time when I thought that medicine was the path [Emeli] would choose to go down," she said, "but she never expressed frustration over the time that it took to get noticed for her music. She started her first gigs in 2006 and broke onto the scene in less than 10 years. It is actually a short time; some people are gigging a lot longer than that before they get the chance to be successful. She was balancing everything. There was the uni degree and she was back and forth to Aberdeen and gigging and finding study time. She has worked hard.

I don't feel she has come on the scene from nowhere. I have had the privilege of seeing that happen. She never let us down. She was a consummate professional even at that age. There was never an issue with her."

McCrum also cites Emeli's level-headedness as a factor in her rise to success. "I wish I could have been there for those first meetings she had with record labels. I don't doubt for a second that she would have charmed them and that they would feel this was someone they could work with. I remember advising her not to let record labels turn her into anything that she was not. She has managed to stay true to herself. That can't be done without having good interpersonal skills, so she has done well. Some people get turned down and give up. Others sign a record deal just for the sake of having a record deal. She didn't do either of those things."

Having taken such an interest in developing Emeli's talent and her career when she was at a young age, David Craig has watched her career develop from afar and admits it has been a humbling experience. "Seeing her on *Later … with Jools Holland* was amazing. I thought 'now doors are going to open and things are going to happen'. "

4. UP A GUMTREE

Another person who recognised Emeli's talent at an early stage of her development as an artist is John Ansdell, a Glaswegian who had started to work with a handful of artists who matched his own musical taste after getting funding support from the Prince's Scottish Youth Business Trust. The charity, which has since merged with the Prince's Trust, was established in the late eighties to help young disadvantaged people in Scotland between the ages of 18 and 25 to set up their own businesses by providing grants of up to £1,000 and loans of up to £5,000. It seems a somewhat paltry amount when one sees the millions spent on marketing alone by entertainment giants such as Time Warner and EMI, but John took advantage of it and was determined to help up-and-coming talent from his base in a flat in the West End of Glasgow.

"Adele, or Emeli as she has come to be known, was just 16 when she met her manager, Adrian," he said. "They stayed in touch, but at the time her focus was on education and medicine. Her management team were around after that, always there or thereabouts, but perhaps they hadn't made a commitment while she was at university, or because that was her first priority."

While working as a part-time after-care assistant for a local primary school, Ansdell contacted Emeli after she placed a call-out on the small ads website Gumtree for help with her career. "I had the idea to start my own label because I loved soul music and hip hop," he said. "I first came across her because she'd posted an ad on Gumtree and quoted all my favourite artists. I had actually done music production as a hobby for six months so I emailed her some of my music that I produced. She liked it so we agreed to meet."

In fact, it was at the MC Guru gig in Edinburgh where Ansdell first saw Emeli perform. "I could tell straight away that she was an incredible talent," he said. "Not only could she sing but she was also a great songwriter and musician – she ticked every box."

Blown away by Emeli's soulful voice and her talent as a songwriter, Ansdell agreed to meet her in Glasgow where she had been booked onto the bill of the Kelvingroove concert at Kelvingrove Park, in the city's West End. The fact they met during a torrential downpour didn't dampen their enthusiasm for making music together.

"It kicked off from there. We hit it off right away and made a very impromptu contract there and then and she became my first signing to the label. I came along and she was delighted to have the chance to make music so long as she could manage it with her studies. Basically, I already knew that she had great tracks because she sent me her MySpace page link. On it were three or four of her songs and they were just incredible. I wanted to give her more focus. Instead of playing the odd gig here and there, I wanted to get a proper launch plan, to get proper artwork made up and a full album recorded, and to see what would happen."

The pair agreed to meet again at Ansdell's nearby flat where they signed a contract to release an album, which Ansdell would executive produce. However, even without his help, there's every likelihood an album of material would have come together. Those who knew Emeli at that time talk of how driven the teenager was, despite the fact that there were no guarantees her efforts would come to anything. Emeli got to work using a software program called Reason, which works as an integrated recording studio that boasts "unlimited audio tracks, million-dollar mixing and a massive collection of sounds".

"She produced the album herself with the help of her friend who had access to a university recording studio," Ansdell said. "She is obviously a talented pianist. She produced an album of material for me on her laptop!"

Once the album, called *Have You Heard?*, was completed, Ansdell set about organising an album launch in Òran Mór, a converted church which dominates the corner of Glasgow's Byres Road and Great Western Road. On Sunday, December 16, 2007, the Scottish edition of the now defunct *News Of The World* ran the details of Adele Sandé's show, albeit buried deep in the listings section. The one-line description cast her as a solo songstress with Nina Simone and Jill Scott influences.

The young music entrepreneur Ansdell had sunk his funding into the launch, paying the musician's full union rates and sparing no expense when it came to making sure the night was a success. However, every good idea has competition.

Within a year, Glasgow would find itself bestowed with the title UNESCO City of Music – a UK first – in recognition of the city's musical heritage and its hotbed of a live music scene, which punches well above its weight for a city with a population of just 600,000. Forget New York; speak to some of the world's greatest entertainers and they'll tell you if you can make it in Glasgow, you can make it anywhere. The same week Emeli – or Adele as she was still known at the time – was due to perform at Òran Mór, Glaswegians were spoiled for musical choice. Rock legends Status Quo, former Fairground Attraction vocalist Eddi Reader, indie-favourite Emma Pollock of the Delgados and up-and-coming rockers Glasvegas all had gigs taking place within a one-mile radius of her show. The Proclaimers, Les McKeown's Legendary Bay City Rollers and Britpop favourites Ocean Colour Scene also had gigs that week. In fact, the city boasts 127 music events *every* week, according to Glasgow's marketing bureau. As such, it might have been easy for Emeli to go unnoticed or for her to find herself singing to a smattering of friends and family. After all, the newspaper's hot pick of the week was not Adele Sandé, but Steven Lindsay, the former frontman of the Big Dish, a band that had enjoyed local and cult success in the eighties. But with Ansdell's entrepreneurial spirit and his strong Glasgow, the Òran Mór album launch was a sell-out, drawing 140 paying customers and a sizeable guest list.

Those who attended got their hands on an extremely limited CD, featuring a handful of Emeli's songs (they actually remained available on iTunes long after she had achieved her dream of chart stardom, to be heard and purchased by anyone savvy enough to search under the name Adele Sandé).

Ansdell said: "There were eight tracks on [the CD]. Seven were tracks she recorded for me and one was a live track she did for the competition at the BBC for Trevor Nelson's show. We pressed up 300 copies ... It was an amazing night – the venue was packed and her performance, backed by a full band, was incredible. The album went to family and friends and a few people who had been at the gig."

Surprisingly, you can't find a single copy of Adele Sandé's *Have You Heard?* on eBay or any other secondary market website. Clearly, those who got their hands on the album have enjoyed the songs enough to want to keep them, rather than sell it for a collector's premium. "I bump into people every now and then who just randomly tell me they were at that concert and have the CD," Ansdell said. "I don't know if it is worth a few bob now and I only have a couple left myself. I had the eight songs we recorded and she had recorded quite a few demos that she laid down in my flat. That's quite nice to have some unique recordings."

Among the tracks on the album are songs such as 'Patchwork', 'Dirty Jeans' and 'Woman's Touch', the track Emeli recorded for Trevor Nelson's *The Lowdown*. "Everything was original," Ansdell said. "We had those 300 CDs made and then we decided to take four of the tracks off it. We took the BBC track off because we weren't sure if we were allowed to have that on there in terms of the copyright, and three other songs that weren't quite full length were taken off too. That left us with an EP's worth of material."

Lorne Cowieson, who played session keyboards for Emeli at the Òran Mór launch, said: "We did the gig, and it was really at the beginning. All her mates came and her family came too because it was going to be her first gig with a full band and lighting on a big stage. She had recorded the record but it was a very low production with samples and there wasn't a band behind the recording to speak of. The band were put together to do this gig."

However, Emeli and Ansdell soon realised it was going to be unsustainable to keep paying the musicians to play further shows, and so the line-up was disbanded.

"The band weren't necessarily the greatest either and I think Emeli recognised that herself," Cowieson claimed. But Emeli wasn't about to let that stop her. "She did the gig, which launched the CD, then she wanted to do full gigs. She and I had struck up a good relationship and when it was time for her to go out and get more gigging experience, that's when she asked me to put together a band for her, and I did. We played the Lemon Tree in Aberdeen and gigs in Glasgow and Stirling. At that stage I was purely the musical director."

However, not all Emeli's appearances were as well received as her album launch. Struggling to find places to play, her gigs included one at the sports bar chain PJ Champs, in Glasgow's West End, where she played to just 50 people who paid little attention and chatted loudly throughout the first four songs. Emeli became so angry that she cut her set short and walked out.

Ansdell said: "The gig was horrendous. Unfortunately, it was my gig. I used to go there every Monday to play pool with a friend after work and the owner suggested I put on music gigs once a month, but I didn't have enough experience in promoting concerts. We did promo and got a few people there, but people talked through her set so she cut things halfway and said it wasn't for her. She did four songs or so in what was supposed to be a half-hour acoustic set. Her songs back then were deep and soulful and people had talked all through it, so it didn't work at all."

Despite Emeli's subsequent success, Ansdell has resisted the temptation to release the EP on CD and cash in on her fame. "My thinking regarding the EP we did together was just to let it be, because it would be blatantly obvious that I would be trying to make money off her success," he said. "I'm not the most wealthy person at all. I still had a lot of debt from when I started and I had a lot of offers. I knocked back everything ... because it didn't quite feel right. But I felt the tracks were so good I wanted people to know they exist. I love those tracks she did. They are more soulful and jazzy, and that's what I'm into. Last time I spoke to Emeli she said those tracks happened a long time ago and that she has moved on to bigger and better things and I got the impression she wasn't too fussed what happened to them."

The duo did, however, make the EP's four tracks – 'Baby's Eyes', 'Best Friends', 'Has Needs' and 'Your Song' – available for digital download on iTunes within a few months of the Òran Mór show, yet few are aware of the EP's existence, let alone how to search for it. "I'd always been torn about what to do with the EP. The launch was a massive success and is still the best night I've had since I got involved in music. The plan had been for Adele, sorry Emeli, to continue with her course and write songs between the beginning of New Year and the following summer, and we'd release more tracks in the summer or just after."

But during that period, Ansdell had taken on other acts, and this left the young entrepreneur overstretched. "In hindsight I shouldn't have done [that] and wish I hadn't because it ate up the remaining budget I had to work with [Emeli]. Unfortunately, the launch used up the majority of the funding and as I had commitments to the other acts, I quickly ran out of money and wasn't able to continue the success we had," Ansdell said. "It was a very frustrating time for me. I tried desperately to find an investor – I spent a year trying to get proper investment – but no one was willing to take a gamble.

The small amount of funding came too late for Ansdell, though once Emeli had found fame, and just days before she was due to pick

up her BRITs Critics' Choice award at the prestigious ceremony
in London, the Scottish *Daily Record*'s website posted a link to the
EP, along with an in-depth article on Ansdell's relationship with the
rising star from Alford.

"It bumped up the listings on the likes of SoundCloud and I noticed
a small increase in download sales on the likes of iTunes and Amazon,"
Ansdell said. "It was a boost. The story got repeated in blogs and in
The Sun. Even publications in places like Seattle and others in the USA
picked up on it. That was great exposure for me. There was interest
from half a dozen different labels. Big ones. I got offers from private
investors who wanted to fund an awareness campaign for a cut of the
sales of the songs. I thought of doing an awareness campaign under my
label Innovation Music, but my preference was for Virgin EMI to take
it on because she is their artist."

Ansdell's association with Emeli remains strong and he admits the
interest in his involvement has given him the perfect platform from
which to develop new artists.

"John is brilliant," Emeli said. "He is a really cool guy. He was a
big supporter. He is great and his whole family are really lovely. It's
brilliant to hear he is working on breaking new acts. I think he'll do
very well."

Ansdell added: "Somebody at STV is interested in doing a
documentary about how I started with [Emeli] and the artists I am
working with now. The one thing I wanted was not to look bitter
and money-grabbing because I am not at all. I could have cashed
in by now but I haven't so far. I get a lot of people contacting me
looking for advice and consultancy work."

Long after Emeli's career took off, Ansdell finally got his own
reward when Virgin EMI stepped in and bought the EP tracks from
him for a high five-figure sum. The label is considering the songs
being available at a future date, which is good news for fans keen to
hear Emeli's early work.

"I'm glad Virgin EMI picked up the songs," Ansdell said. "The fact
that Emeli's label now has the songs seems fitting. It has helped me to

pay off my debts built up from recording studio costs and maybe buy a shirt and a pair of socks into the bargain, and that's all that really matters. The great thing is that I know Emeli will be happy.

"It also gave me a credibility that enabled me to attend meetings on a level with others in the industry. The two least established acts on my label, Sunshine Social and Aaron Fyfe, have albums that are sounding incredible. The feedback I have had so far is outstanding. I'm looking forward to starting a promotional campaign with them and trying to get some support down south as well. The goal is to get them a deal with a major label. I have to put in a bit of groundwork before they'll consider a new act."

This coming from the man who signed Emeli Sandé.

Meanwhile, Emeli's relationship with keyboard player Lorne Cowieson had been bubbling away, to the point where the pair became the duo known as Adele Sandé & Lorne Cowieson. One of their first performances as a two-piece took place at the Junction Café in the Scottish village of Lochwinnoch. "I think we got our dinner. I can't remember if we got paid. If we did, it was £20, our dinner and a bottle of wine," he recalls. "I play at a high level but it's not about the money. We were just making music. She was trying to get her confidence up in terms of performance, though it's incredible how confident she was and how good her voice was considering she hadn't done much performing.

"She was absolutely brilliant to work with. We struck up what I thought was a pretty good friendship. We started working together as a duo with me on piano and Emeli singing. We played restaurants including one in the village where I live. She was singing jazz standards and her own songs. Even from rehearsing with her, it was a case of her being a one-take wonder: she just nailed things. It was obvious she was capable of being pretty big. Eighty per cent of the songs were her own and they were good songs. She was impressive, and everyone who heard her was aware that she was destined for stardom. We played the gig at the Junction. Everyone from the village giggles about it now. When she did the Olympics they were all saying 'I remember when she played the Junction'. That was the height of when we were working as a duo."

As well as the small-time gigs, Cowieson would record demos of Emeli's songs at his home in Lochwinnoch and her flat in Glasgow, recordings that would later make their way into the hands of various record label executives.

"I can't overplay it. I could say I was helping her write her songs. I was, but only because I knew maybe a bit more about jazz harmonies," Cowieson, who currently plays with the Scottish National Jazz Orchestra, said. "There were certain sounds she liked, certain Stevie Wonder inflections that she liked, but she didn't know how to make them. We would just tweak the harmonies a little bit and put in some chord extensions. She used to say she would bring her songs to me to be 'Stevie'd'. I don't want to underplay what I did but I don't want to overplay it either, because I wasn't writing the songs with her. The songs came finished. She did all the lyrics and the melody. I would say, why don't you put a ninth on top of that chord and she would say that was a good sound. It would help to flesh out some of the sounds she wanted."

Just as Adele took her duties as chief songwriter seriously, even then she was smart enough to know that she ought to have top billing. "It was Adele Sandé & Lorne Cowieson. I remember we had both our pictures on the poster, but it would be Adele Sandé in big letters and Lorne Cowieson in little letters. At the time more people would have heard of me in Glasgow than had heard of her, but obviously that's changed."

A working musician for 18 years, Cowieson had originally been recommended to Emeli as a local musician who could play jazz and world music. "Pop music was something I wasn't interested in until Emeli came along. The strength of her songs and what she wanted to do with her harmonies and the fact that she was doing Nina Simone-style jazz standards was amazing. She fancied herself as a bit of a jazz singer and perhaps when she is older that's something she'll go back to. The skills I had made us a good match and helped her to develop what she wanted to do. There's no way I was teaching her how to sing. That was already there.

"I just really liked actually hanging out with her and rehearsing. The full band stuff was good, but I just really liked taking my piano up to her house and singing and recording. Her voice is amazing and it made it easy to play piano and it made the recording process really easy. I enjoyed adding harmonically to the songs. It was a very creative and productive time. We did most of the recordings at mine because I had a proper home studio and we did bits and bobs at hers. We practised and rehearsed. I wasn't star-struck. It was just this lassie who was studying medicine and who was a great singer."

However much Cowieson enjoyed having such a lassie to work with, he would later discover the writing was on the wall for him when the music publishing deal came through within two years. "She didn't have good demos of a lot of her songs, so we recorded demos of voice and piano of all her main songs and the jazz standards. She took those to London and used them to get the interviews with the music publishing companies. She had to sing live for them, but the demos got her foot in the door. ...then she got signed. I had plans to keep connections but I got cut out," he said. "It's such a shame it wasn't able to continue, but I guess that's what happens when you get swallowed up by the whole London thing and a big label who probably told her who to work with.

"She said she'd got a really good contract and at that time she was still planning to finish her medical degree. She was heading down to London a lot and she had said to her publishers that she was still going to be living in Scotland. She told them she had been working away with me and that she wanted me to be involved, but I think that was possible when she was staying in Scotland and finishing her degree. I never spoke to her again, because soon after that she had decided to chuck university and move to London. Obviously it's a disappointment when you feel that you have come close to something and it doesn't happen for you, but I can't hold it against

Emeli. It was her talent, her voice and her songs and her everything that was pushing it."

Cowieson is at pains to stress that he holds no ill feeling towards Emeli's decision to carry on without him. "It wasn't me that went on to get signed to Virgin Records. It was her. She goes down to London and you don't know what pressures are being put on her. 'What, you've got a middle-aged white guy who plays the keyboards? No, we're not interested in that. We'll sort you out.' They sign the cheques after all. I'm not negative about it. I enjoyed the time and the experience I got. How many musicians have stories of working with someone famous at some point? She moved to London where there are all these other incredible musicians and arrangers around her that she is able to work with. Fair enough."

Long before she had a publishing deal under her belt, Emeli was also to prove herself willing to pay her dues with any kind of concert available to her, no matter how small. Having previously played the Junction Café in the village of Lochwinnoch, she formed a new band from musicians who had turned up to see her at another café bar, led by a friend of her boyfriend, Adam Gouraguine.

"The first time I ever saw her was in Mono near Trongate," Dade Thomas, recalls. "She played there. I'd heard her CD so I went along."

Thomas, a student at the University of Glasgow before going on to study at Glasgow's Strathclyde university, had no sooner arrived at the tiny Mono café than he bumped into the tall, handsome Montenegrin. He and Gouraguine had played basketball together for the university and their team had won a British University Sports Association award. "I knew Adam, now Emeli's husband, before I went to Mono," Thomas said. "When I turned up at the gig, I didn't know Adam was her man. It was one of those small-world situations. I said to him, 'What the hell Adam, what are you doing here?' It helped to break the ice."

Thomas had turned up at the gig with the intention of persuading Emeli to let him form her new band. And he had an ace up his sleeve to help him get his way; he filmed the Mono gig so his bandmates could study Emeli's songs ahead of her arrival at their first rehearsal.

Thomas' fellow students, Michael Abubakar, Alan Langdon and Leo Forde, were delighted to get the chance to be in the band. A BA Applied Music student at Strathclyde university at that time, Abubakar had accompanied Thomas to see Emeli play Mono. The Glasgow-based musician, who has since toured with the likes of Dan Reed and Pearl & the Puppets and who also advertises his services as a piano tutor, recalled: "I started playing with her when I was in second year in uni. I was doing the music course at Strathclyde university and one of my friends on the course, Dade Thomas, said to me that he had heard about this singer who was totally great. She was playing Mono and we went down there to see her. Twenty or 30 people were there to watch her play with the jazz band she was working with at the time."

Abubakar recalls that Emeli had yet to settle on the musical style which would lead to millions of sales within the next few years, but he was suitably impressed to want to join her on keyboards. "The songs she was playing then were different to the songs that made it onto her album," he said. "After the gig, Dade asked if she ever needed a band, to get in touch."

Nobody was more surprised than Abubakar when Emeli contacted Thomas just a couple of weeks later. He invited her to drop by for a rehearsal at the university in the evenings after their studies. Abubakar said: "Dade had filmed the gig that night on his video camera. We watched the DVD and listened to what those musicians were doing and learned the parts from that so that when she came to that first rehearsal, we already knew the songs. She was quite impressed that we had learned it all from filming her that night. It's not as easy as listening to recordings ... I think that's why we ended up doing quite a few gigs with her."

Abubakar describes the setup at the rehearsal rooms in the university as being nothing fancy. "We were in uni all day playing anyway and she would come up in the evening. We rehearsed upstairs in one of the rehearsal rooms we used quite a lot. There are tiny piano rooms and slightly bigger rooms where you can set up a small band, then two or three bigger rooms for the jazz orchestra. We used one of the medium-sized rooms upstairs. It was a basic setup. I used one keyboard. No synths. At that point the songs were quite different. It suited basic instruments. The sound she has now is obviously more commercial, but the sound back then was more of a neo-soul vibe, like Jill Scott. We did that leading up to our first gigs."

Abubakar took on keyboards, Dade Thomas became the drummer, Alan Langdon played bass, and Leo Forde completed the line-up on guitar. "That was the first line-up of that band, which was four of us from that same course in uni," Abubakar said.

In the initial weeks after the band formed, Thomas had an idea for a show that he hoped would appeal to Emeli's good nature and benefit his church: a fundraiser in the dinner hall of his old school. "I had a charity fundraiser for my church, which is the TEAM church. It stands for the Everlasting Arms Ministries," Thomas said. "I asked Emeli to please come along and sing at it. That was at Hillhead High School."

As soon as Emeli agreed to play Hillhead High School (again, like so many of those early gigs, it took place in Glasgow's West End), Dade got down to persuading his old music teacher at the school, Ian Matheson, to put on the gig.

"Dade hadn't long left school when he came back and asked if he could hold a fundraising concert," Matheson, who still teaches at the school, said. "I told him to go ahead and organise it since it was his thing. They rehearsed with Emeli for a couple of days and that was it. The event took place the next week. It was like an old Diana Durbin movie, where one minute they are planning and the next minute they have the show."

Less than 80 or so people crowded into the cafeteria, purchasing drinks and snacks as they arrived to help boost the church's coffers. They politely munched away as Emeli and the backing band, former pupils who'd eaten their school dinner countless times at the tables they were now playing to, put on a great show.

Abubakar said: "It was nice to do a gig at the high school because we hadn't seen our music teacher and the other teachers who taught us since we had left to go to university."

Thomas added: "We did about five songs and the gig went really well. People liked it and enjoyed it. It was a hundred per cent the opposite of the sort of gigs she does now. There were 50 to 80 people there. We ticketed it and we raised about £400 or £500, because people also made donations and we were selling cans, muffins and chocolates."

Having given his blessing for the show to go ahead, Matheson attended and he was impressed with the performance. "They played in the wee dinner hall that doubles as our theatre. It has a wee stage in there with curtains so she really was singing in the dinner hall. The songs she performed were not in the same style she has become known for. They were more involved and musically complicated, which appealed to me. I remember being asked if I had heard of her and I was told that she was going to have a great career and that she was writing with Cheryl Cole."

But before stardom beckoned, there was the small matter of a fellow female rising star with the same name standing in the way.

Adele Adkins was born in Tottenham, north London, on May 5, 1988. Her father walked out when she was two, leaving her 20-year-old mother, Penny Adkins, to bring her up alone. By the age of four, Adele was already obsessed with singing; by 2006, she was graduating from the BRIT School for Performing Arts & Technology. After a friend posted her demo on MySpace, Adele attracted the attention of Nick Huggett at XL Records, and by September that year he had signed her.

The following year Adele became the first recipient of the BRITs Critics' Choice award. In January 2008, she enjoyed her first Top 10 hit with the song 'Chasing Pavements' and her spectacular debut album, *19* (named after the age she was when she wrote most of its songs), debuted at number one a week later. The album was nominated for the 2008 Mercury Music Prize and four Grammys: Record of the Year, Song of the Year, Best Female Vocal Performance for 'Chasing Pavements' and Best New Artist, of which she went on to win the latter two. It was fair to say that Adele (she dropped her surname for her onstage persona) had arrived.

Which led to a dilemma for the up-and-coming Adele Sandé. Until then, she was beginning to make a name for herself with her given name, but when 'the other Adele' hit big, she had a decision to make: if the record labels in London were to take her seriously, she'd have to change her name. She chose Rio Sandé.

"She was experimenting with her name," Cowieson said. "I don't know what Rio was all about, but I heard that she had to change her name because the other Adele was much more famous. They are equal now in terms of their fame."

John Ansdell said: "For a while [Emeli] was determined to go with Rio Sandé. I tried to tell her that was a bad idea, but she was set on it at the time."

It soon became clear that the new name was just as baffling. "People kept confusing Rio Sandé and Rio Grande," Emeli said, "I was Rio Sandé for one week. I did one gig There's one flyer... My mum rang me up. She says, 'I don't think this is gonna work'."

Oxford-based DJ and blogger Kid Fury blogged about Emeli while she was still a fourth-year medical student. He'd championed Adele Sandé, approaching record labels, including Sony, and attempting to get one of her tracks included in a soul CD compilation of up-and-coming talent. As it happens, he failed on both fronts, but this didn't stop him from proclaiming in his blog that Adele Sandé had a massive future ahead of her. And so did her sisters. When he heard about Rio and Emeli Sandé [Adele Sandé's middle name], he wondered why they had not teamed up with their sibling, Adele. Three incredible singers from the same family with such soulful voices would surely prove irresistible.

He blogged: "Currently in her fourth-year as a medical student at Glasgow uni, I feel that Ms Sandé, although delivering great hooks on her two breakthrough singles, has so much more to offer and I feel like the evidence has been covered up, as seen in the acoustic piano soul gems that graced her MySpace page. 'Diamond Rings' is the only track in the media player so you will have to take my word that if indeed Emeli Sandé is definitely an artist, in a perfect world she would be on that Leona Lewis & Alexandra Burke paper (without the reality show) and boy if her, Adele and Rio (whom i just stumbled across) are sisters .... WACK SINGERS ARE VERY MUCH IN DANGER!!!."

The only problem was all three 'sisters' were the same person.

Kid Fury, real name Franklin Humphrey, said: "When I first came across her it was on MySpace. I'd [seen] a couple of acoustic videos she had done. Initially, I thought Adele and Emeli were these amazing twin sisters. I thought that it would make sense for them to be a group. The Sandés or something. The three of them – Emeli, Rio and Adele – would have been amazing. In the end, I was told Adele Adkins had such a big hit that it would be confusing for [her and Emeli] to have the same name, and that Emeli had changed her name a couple of times.

"I was naive enough to think the whole world was noticing that we had this amazing artist," he said. "I was working for Soulfood Promotions at Sony and they kept asking me about up-and-coming hip hop and R&B artists and I did mention her several times, but I felt like nobody was listening to me. They all thought they knew it all. I remember pushing my bosses to listen, but they ignored me. I'd be ranting on about her videos I'd seen on YouTube. Nobody was convinced, but I was. When I still believed Emeli, Rio and Adele were sisters, I pitched her to everybody I knew that was asking about soul artists. I kept on telling people she was the best girl I had heard. Every time I spoke to someone I would ask if they had heard of the Sandé sisters or Sandé twins. I didn't know which one to pitch. But when nobody listened to me, that was disheartening. They thought, Franklin is talking rubbish again, basically."

In March of 2009, Emeli was still being billed as "up-and-coming singer Rio Sandé" when she opened for Senegalese musician Samba

Sene at another charity fundraiser in Glasgow. The show, advertised as "a night of soul, African and Reggae music", took place at the city's intimate Admiral Bar, and she also shared billing with DJs Tchico and Jeremiyah. Sene, who had moved to Edinburgh from the west African country of Senegal in 1999 and who continues to perform gigs around Scotland, turned up at the city centre bar just as Rio Sandé was singing the last song in her short, though enjoyable, set. Still an unknown and having only recently decided on the name change, Rio Sandé was a new experience for the audience that night. But it didn't take long for them to realise they were being treated to someone with a special talent and a wonderful voice. Despite arriving just as she was approaching the end of her set, Samba Sene was also impressed.

He said: "One of my friends, the DJ Jeremiyah, who used to live here in Edinburgh, put on the concert, so I offered to come along and perform. We had come from Edinburgh that night. The concert wasn't full, but it wasn't empty either. The dance floor was busy and Emeli got a good reception when she finished her set. We all applauded. Everyone did. I am surrounded by good musicians and I know one when I see one."

Once again Emeli's parents had been helping move her career along.

"I hadn't met Emeli before but her mum and dad had been in touch," Sene explained. "They had seen me on MySpace and contacted me to say they had a daughter who was young and singing and that they would love me to meet her. When the gig happened, her mum and dad were there. They had come to see her."

Sene enjoyed her performance so much he introduced himself to Emeli and invited her to join him during his headline performance. She didn't hesitate. Despite the fact that the pair had never met until that night and with no rehearsal having taken place beforehand, she accompanied Sene (who was performing under the band name Diwan with keyboard player Khadim Thiam and Madoune N'Diaye on the sabar, a traditional drum played in Senegal as well as Gambia) on his final song, 'Africa'.

Sene said of the performance: "Emeli had not heard the song 'Africa' before and I hadn't seen her before. She came onstage with me and sang along to my song. From the first moment I saw her I realised this was a very talented girl. She was hanging out with a keyboard player I know who is also very talented and when I saw her with him, I knew that she was something."

Emeli's keyboard player, Michael Abubakar, picks up the story. "I knew Samba was playing … at that point, it was the kind of music I was really into. Myself and Dade thought it was great that anyone was even playing that kind of music in Glasgow. I think I still have that gig on DVD somewhere because somebody filmed it that night. That gig was really good fun. It was somebody's birthday because I remember [Emeli] singing 'Happy Birthday' at the end. Samba invited us all up to play at the end of the gig and then we all sang 'Happy Birthday'. We all ended up onstage together, playing. Samba is the kind of guy who will invite you up even if you haven't heard the song before, so it doesn't surprise me that it happened that way on the night. We all knew how good at that point she was, but we never imagined that in the blink of an eye she would go on to become a global superstar."

Looking back, Samba believes that night gave Emeli a much-needed confidence boost. "At the time, I was doing a tour of Edinburgh, Glasgow and Aberdeen," he said. "I remember thinking that [the Admiral Bar] wasn't a big venue ... I thought it was so small but even so, the atmosphere was good and everybody loved it. Everybody went home happy. I haven't met her since that night. I have seen her on TV. I was happily surprised to see her do so well but not shocked because I knew she had talent. I felt it straight away when I walked into that room, I felt something. I was like, whoa. She can sing."

Samba's manager Morag Neil said: "They did the song together and she was great. The audience loved it and it was a nice crowd that night. She hadn't had a complete image makeover until after that when she had the haircut, and that made her stand out. "

Rio Sandé may have been an unknown to the audience members that night at the Admiral Bar, but elsewhere she was picking up steam and a little more recognition.

"Even though nobody knew who she was as a solo artist, she was already writing songs for loads of different people at that point. I remember her coming in to uni one day and telling me, 'Man, I've just been asked to write a song for Jamelia'. We said, 'That's cool. Do you want to let us hear it?' So she sat down to the piano and she played it for us. I remember thinking it totally sounded like a Jamelia song. I'd never heard of anyone being asked to write for an artist and come out with a song that sounded as if that artist had written it and which was totally perfect for that artist. I remember thinking that Emeli totally knew what she was doing with her songwriting. That was really impressive."

Thomas was also impressed by Emeli's generosity of spirit. "On a personal level, she was really encouraging," he said. "Sometimes we'd all write songs together. She would invite Michael and I up to her place to hang out and to write some music. I thought that was really cool of her. She encouraged me as a songwriter. She always showed an interest. We used to do just sit and write. We would take one of my songs and all sing over it. We'd do the same with each other's songs. If I had written a hook around a chorus, I would sing, then we would all write lyrics over the same part. We would go in a circle. She would change the melody and rewrite the song, then Michael would do the same. That was really fun. I was in my shell a bit but she would make me sing to bring me out of it."

Since she was struggling to make ends meet as a student and was unable to pay session wages, Emeli was grateful to Thomas and the others, who played with her for the love of the music. Thomas said: "I had no problem playing for free for Emeli. I understand that at the initial stages of a venture there isn't the money to pay band members. It was just great playing her music. I loved it and had no problem with that."

"I'm playing for singers and doing what I can to make a living," Abubakar said. "I remember being in Berkeley at one point and having to jump between a rehearsal with Katie [Sutherland] – who was still Pearl & the Puppets – and Adele. If I think people are really good I will work with them for free, because I see a future in it."

But their hard work would soon pay off, in a string of gigs far more prestigious than their usual dinner halls and late bars.

Emeli landed a major support slot for May 2009. Solange Knowles, sister to Beyoncé and a successful soul and R&B singer in her own right, came to Glasgow as part of her tour to promote her second album, *Sol-Angel And The Hadley St. Dreams*. "Most of the gigs we did for no money, apart from a gig we did with Solange Knowles," Thomas said. "We got paid for that one."

The show would take place on May 27, 2009 at Òran Mór, the venue at which Adele Sandé had held her album launch in December 2007. Only this time, she had settled on her new stage name. "I went for my middle name, Emeli."

With the help of Dade Thomas, the newly christened Emeli also enlisted three female backing singers – Unoma, Stephanie Lawrence and Dade's sister, Lewa – to reinforce the production values for the special show with Solange. Other new members drafted in for the show included a guitar player from London and a DJ, who played samples and ran some programming. The band would also embark on a mini Scottish tour around the same time.

Rehearsals progressed for both productions in Glasgow's Berkeley 2 Studios, a facility that has been used in the past by touring acts such as Beyoncé, Grace Jones and Iggy Pop, and some of Glasgow's finest including the Blue Nile, Simple Minds and Biffy Clyro. It is hard to believe that on any one day at the rehearsal facility, tucked between industrial complexes in the city centre and a few feet from the River Clyde, Beyoncé could be in one room and guitar legend Slash in another. But having been in existence for over a quarter of a century, Berkeley 2 boasts state-of-the-art equipment, variable lighting and air-conditioned rooms. It was certainly a major step up for the fledgling band.

"We rehearsed in Berkeley for 10 days straight before the tour," Abubakar said. "We didn't know the two new guys from London and ended up doing gigs around Scotland with them. It was just a short tour of Scotland and [Emeli's] first ever tour. It was relatively small venues. It was King Tut's in Glasgow, Electric Circus in Edinburgh and the Lemon Tree in Aberdeen. Her family would always be there to lend support. The first night of the tour was in Dundee on November 12," he continued. "My mum had got me a Diesel watch for my 21st birthday, so I remember the date. I left it in the hotel and Emeli's parents brought it down to the gig in Glasgow at King Tut's a few days later and surprised her with the visit."

Abubakar also has fond memories of the Solange gig. "That was probably just before anything was released," he said, "but around the time, [Emeli] had released the song with Chipmunk and it was before she released anything as a solo artist. We did a medley of four or five songs at the gig where she said, 'For those of you who don't know who I am you might have heard me on all these different songs', which is quite cool. She was really into performance. She just loved gigging. That was the first bigger gig we did with her because it was a big support gig. It was almost sold out and was really good fun."

During this period, Emeli also somehow found the time to make a record that would be sold all over the world – and she would do it old school. Try to get hold of that 7-inch vinyl single today, however, and you'll be hard pushed to find it. Only 500 were printed and vinyl is rarely uploaded digitally, making it even harder to track down an audio file online.

DJ Mark Robb is heavily involved with both Glasgow's Rio Café venue and the soul label Starla Records. Starla specialises in soul, jazz and funk releases – usually old-style 45rpm seven-inch vinyl singles that are distributed in small numbers around the world. Each release comes in a tartan sleeve, chosen partly in an effort to appeal to a Japanese market that has been receptive to the Scottish music scene ever since the tartan-clad Bay City Rollers caused fan hysteria in Japan (and worldwide) in the seventies. Since then cult Scottish bands like the Jesus and Mary Chain, BMX Bandits and Belle & Sebastian have gone on to do well in the land of the rising sun.

Among the Starla Records releases that have appealed to the Japanese is 'SRC 1002' by the DT6, a group consisting of local jazz and soul musicians. The double A-side includes one enjoyable and hypnotic track called '(Theme From) The Baden Persuader', and a link can be found for a low-budget promo video on the label's website. Less than 2,000 people have watched the video on YouTube at the last count, but there is no video for the flip-side track featuring Emeli. Billed as Emeli Sandé & Marco with the DT6, the track was recorded at Marco Rea's Barne Studio in Clydebank, West Dunbartonshire. The production had come about through Lorne Cowieson. "He had recorded [Emeli] singing on his phone when she was playing piano," Robb recalled. "They were looking for gigs at the Rio Café. For a while she was called Rio Sandé. She had taken that name on for a couple of gigs after changing it from her first name because it would mean two Adeles. So it was through Lorne, who wanted to record with her because she had a great voice. He took her to the Barne Studios and Marco did a full session with her. After she got the chance to play at the Rio Café, we were looking for some backing singers on one of our tracks by the DT6, who were recording with us around 2006, 2007. It was a track called 'Takes', recorded in Clydebank with my fellow label producer and engineer, Marco. He sang the lead vocal and Emeli sings on it too as a duet. She was a really nice girl and still studying at Glasgow university at the time. It was great to work with her. She looked different to the way she looks now. She had more of a soul look, including an Afro, back then."

Marco Rea was so impressed by Emeli that he ended up inviting her to work on further songs to fill the session time. "It was just at that point she was changing her name to Emeli," Rea explained. "I wasn't sure what was going on with Emeli when I was working with her. I didn't realise that she had so much going on in the background.

Emeli had been singing with a couple of friends who came up with the idea of her working with my band DT6. I met her through Allan McKeown, who is in the DT6 with me, because Emeli had been performing in Glasgow with a few of the guys involved with Starla. The idea also came up because she was such an amazing singer to get her to be on one of our productions.

"She had written a cracking song called 'Movin''. That was a song that was unreleased, but she had done a vocal for it and I had written a song and we thought it would work fantastic as a duet. There was another song that was never released that we wrote together. Myself, the other guys and Emeli wrote it in the studio as well as recording the song 'Takes'. We sat around the piano and wrote that track together. It has a Motown or Northern Soul feel to it. We had a piano and vocal and since then a backing track has formed. It is unfinished but sounds great. The session for the second song happened in the Barne while we were recording the main track, 'Takes', which Allan and myself had written. We decided to release it as a double A-side because it was starting to cook."

Marco hopes the other song he worked on with Emeli during that session will one day see the light of day. "It would be fantastic to do something with that. Emeli is so busy, but I would love to finish that track, because it is such a brilliant song. The writing session was great. Most of 'Takes' was down and it was easy to bring the vocals to it. That was the last piece of production that was needed. It was really nice to watch her in process. She is a brilliant piano player and has such an amazing voice. It was lovely to throw ideas about. She is a nice person to write a song with. She is very open. The vibes were good in the studio that day and it flowed really nice."

Among those who took an interest in the song once it was released was Tom Moulton. Dubbed the "father of the disco mix", having been responsible for the first continuous-mix album side (on Gloria Gaynor's album *Never Can Say Goodbye*), and produced the first three Grace Jones albums, Moulton had also remixed one of Marco Rea's previous tracks, 'Open My Eyes'. He perked up on hearing the latest song from the Starla label. Rea said: "Tom loved the track I did with Emeli and gave it the thumbs up. He thought the musicianship on the track was fantastic and he loved the vocals as well."

Mark Robb said: "It did well on the jazz, soul and funk scene. Tom was a fan of the track and interested in remixing it. He was very interested in our version of it. He liked it as a soul track."

Within weeks of release the song soon began picking up airplay on specialist radio programmes. Comedian and presenter Mark Lamarr played it on his late-night BBC Radio 2 show, *God's Jukebox*.

The track also caught the attention of actor and DJ Craig Charles, who played it on his hugely influential *Funk And Soul Show* on BBC Radio 6. Charles is probably best known for playing the loveable rogue Dave Lister in the long-running science fiction sitcom *Red Dwarf* in the eighties and nineties, and as *Coronation Street*'s Lloyd Mullaney in 2005/6. But it is his love of soul, jazz and funk music which has given him a second career as a radio presenter and DJ. It's not unusual to find him championing obscure soul cuts that sell in the hundreds rather than thousands and his patronage must have helped the Starla Records release.

"The response to the single was brilliant," Rea said. "DJs were playing the 'Baden Persuader' track and it became a collector's item quickly. With Emeli being on it, the single took off. We did well from it. Most of the 45s we put out get to the right market. Getting from record to record is a success for a small label, but that one in particular did well. They sold in Japan and America. People seem to find these singles in the strangest corners of the universe. The single sold worldwide in a small way. I once saw the single sell for £20 on eBay. I thought I had better hold on to my copy. It's a rarity."

"We sold out of the single," Robb said. "Not a lot of people know it was Emeli Sandé. We're a local not-for-profit cooperative doing it for enjoyment. It is really for our own pleasure of having locally made jazz, soul and funk. We make records as a labour of love. We sell them and get enough money to make another record. Marco is full time in the music scene in Glasgow. It's a hobby and a love of the music.

"It wasn't long after the record sold out that I saw [Emeli] on TV and realised it was that girl who had been up at the studio not so long ago. She had a fantastic talent. Unlike so many others, she was affable and unassuming, humble and a nice person. I hope that is still the same. I'm sure it will be. She seemed very strong in her own mind."

By now, people were starting to notice a change in Emeli, from shy and withdrawn young lady to a self-assured woman. One member of the Berkeley 2 staff, who has asked to remain anonymous, believes she and another Scot who has gone on to have incredible success both had a similar demeanour. "The really weird thing is there are two people I've met over the past seven or eight years who just had this thing where they didn't particularly interact with you, weren't particularly rude in doing so," he said. "They just had what you would describe as a faraway look in their eyes. You felt there was much more to come from them and there was that feeling they could get round everything and nothing would be an issue. The two people were Emeli Sandé and Calvin Harris. There was a quietness. When I met them they were nothing at all and hadn't sold a record. They probably didn't have a penny in their pocket, but you just think they'll find a place for themselves. You very rarely see it, but I saw that in Calvin and I saw it in Emeli. Emeli definitely had it. She didn't really care much about her environment. She seemed unaffected by the things going on around her. There was a slight bubble about her. Whatever things were thrown at her she would deal with them."

He added: "Presumably she is an extremely bright girl. We all know that she was studying to be a doctor. Back then she seemed to think, I might just do something. But there was no arrogance about her, just an impressive confidence."

Dade Thomas has a simple explanation. "Emeli never had the talent problem that some musicians have. She never struggled on ability. She just had to learn to navigate the industry and its politics. That may have knocked her back a wee bit. She got turned down by certain record labels and that must have given her some doubts, but she knew, and rightly so, that no one else is really as good as she is. Vocally she is great but I believe her confidence is in her songwriting ability. In terms of songwriting, she has the wow factor, and combining the two makes her incredible. She can command what she wants because she has those abilities."

Looking back, Dade also believes that Emeli's growing self-confidence was a sign that she could sense her big break wasn't far off. "She was quietly confident, definitely," he said. "It was just her demeanour. She had something about her. She wasn't fussy the way other people are. She was calm."

To this day, Michael Abubakar believes he was in the presence of greatness even in those early days of Emeli's career. "She was a lot of fun to work with. Her songwriting and her voice always stood out for me. It will be hard to work with someone again with a voice like that. It's so impeccable all the time. She never ever sings flat," he says. "Even in rehearsals when she was tired, the quality of her voice was unbelievable. On the tour at the Electric Circus in Edinburgh her in-ear monitors broke or fell out and she wasn't able to hear herself sing, but I had her voice pumped through my monitor and she never missed a note. Everything was bang on all the way through the show."

Despite building a close working relationship with her band members, according to Abubakar, Emeli generally kept her dreams and aspirations to herself. "I really liked working with her. When we rehearsed she was quite businesslike and got down to getting the work done. We talked. Obviously when you are away on tour, you are in the van every day so we talked about things, but I can't ever remember her talking about her goals or anything like that. She was sure of what she wanted to do, but you could tell that she was never being pushed in any direction by management that she didn't want to go. She was very specific about the way she wanted her songs to be and she stuck with that. That has definitely worked for her. That's important in this business especially if you are a new artist in this industry, which is so cut-throat. There are so many people who will tell you different things, but she was very honest with herself and her approach to things was very good.

"Style-wise, the music was very different from when I started playing with her until the end of our time together, and the last tour especially. By the end, the songs were more like they are now. You can never take the soul away from her music because she has a huge voice and it is a very soulful voice. The music became a lot more accessible and it reached a wider range of people. A lot of the tunes like 'Daddy' and tunes that made it onto the album *Our Version Of Events* were all being played on the tour. She was probably already deciding which ones were going to be put on the album."

5. DEAL OR NO DEAL

While an increasing number of musicians in Scotland were thrilled to be working with someone they suspected was destined for success, Emeli remained determined to become a doctor, and it was to Tordzro, the CEO and artistic director of Pan African Arts Scotland, she turned, having decided she wanted to move to Africa where she intended to find work.

"There was a time when she was interested in doing a placement in Ghana so I got in touch with some people in the medical profession there," Tordzro said. "As a medical student at that time, she wanted to go abroad to work in some hospitals in Ghana and she had asked me to arrange contacts for her. It was towards the latter part of her studies. She had plans to go there and she was excited about it, but that didn't happen and she did not go to Ghana in the end because she changed her mind."

Emeli sensed her luck was about to improve. A year in Ghana might put her musical aspirations in jeopardy just as she was beginning to build momentum. Instead, Emeli spent time closer to home, in Madrid, Spain, on a medical placement scheme. During this time her mum sent a CD of her songs to BBC Radio 1Xtra. Ras Kwame played the disc as part of his Homegrown Sessions, which led to

Emeli becoming one of four artists to be invited to play at a showcase in Soho, London.

On July 7, 2008, around 100 people turned up to hear the latest urban acts looking to get spotted at London's fortnightly showcase, I Love Live with 1Extra, held at the Favela Chic nightclub in hip Shoreditch. Among those in the audience was Shahid Khan, an aspiring producer and songwriter who had built his own recording equipment with money he'd won on the TV game show *Deal Or No Deal* two years earlier. Those who've seen the Channel 4 television show, hosted by Noel Edmonds, will know it's a game of chance in which a single contestant tries to outwit the Banker by opening one of 22 identical sealed boxes over the course of several rounds. The boxes conceal randomly assigned sums of money ranging from 1p to £250,000. The contestant chosen at the start of the show brings his box to the table. He then selects to open the remaining boxes in an order of his choosing, while the banker offers a 'deal' of real money in return for the contents of the contestant's own box. The contestant may agree to take the deal at any point, rather than risk walking home with a derisory sum, or choose to open all 22 boxes and gamble on the contents of their own being a better deal. Eventually, having made 26 appearances on the show during which he opened boxes for other contestants, Shahid took centre stage. He opened box after box before Noel Edmonds asked him "Shahid Khan, a self-employed music producer, deal or no deal?" for the final time. Shahid answered "Deal!" and walked away with £44,000. Grateful for the cash, he ploughed it into recording equipment set up in his garden shed and formed Naughty Boy productions.

For two years, Shahid had practised his craft, laying down beats and occasionally tracks by unknown rappers before turning up at 1Extra's I Love Live that night in the hope of discovering new talent. Shahid had no idea that Emeli Sandé would be opening. In fact, in 2008, Emeli was still known as Adele Sandé; she wasn't on anyone's radar, and the small crowd paid little attention to her as she performed.

Shahid, who by then had adopted the street moniker Naughty Boy, was the exception.

"She performed one song and I was amazed by her. It definitely felt like we were meant to meet that night," he said. "I had just been working with some rappers in the scene, like Chipmunk and Tinie Tempah. Everyone was still relatively underground. They hadn't been signed and I had just started. At the time, the showcase I Love Live was really small. It didn't have a profile. I was invited there to see someone else. I didn't know who Emeli was. She was Adele Sandé then anyway. I watched her perform and […] it felt like she was just singing to me in the room. Obviously she wasn't because there was other people there, but I did feel a connection. I just couldn't believe what I was seeing. I spoke to her after she came offstage, but nobody else went up to her afterwards, even though she was amazing. It can't have been that they were shy because she wasn't known or anything. Emeli was the first person I met on my journey to becoming a producer."

Determined to impress this fresh talent, Naughty Boy told Emeli he'd worked with Bashy, a London-based grime artist of Jamaican and Dominican descent who had released a handful of mix tapes. "She told me she was going back to Scotland the next day," he said. "I was a bit shy, but I asked her to come into my car so that I could play her some music."

Emeli sought out her sister, Lucy, who had come along to support her on the night, and the two girls followed Naughty Boy outside to his Peugeot 306. He rifled through the glove compartment and popped a CD into the player. "We didn't even know each other and I was playing her music. Her sister had heard of Bashy and it just felt nice. Both of us had a feeling that we should stay in touch and work together. She has told me she felt the same as me. What I love about it is this business is controlled and sessions are put together. But me and Emeli happened in as natural a way as possible," he said. "We were both trying to do something and all we did was trust that we should do it together."

Describing the meeting as her big break, Emeli said: "He had been trying to build up his name as a producer and asked if I wanted to work with him. We got in the studio and we clicked, work-wise. I just really enjoyed listening to what he was doing. It was so different from other people's stuff. We just started writing, not necessarily for me. It took the music to something completely original. It took me out of my jazz piano niche, and it took him out of his urban scene. We just thought, 'Let's write a pop tune and experiment.'"

At first Emeli wrote songs from her student flat in Glasgow and sent them by email to Naughty Boy in London. Without record company backing, it was up to Naughty Boy to pay for Emeli to fly to London by Easyjet. For the first six months of their working relationship, she commuted the 800-mile round trip on alternate weekends, staying at a B&B round the corner from Ealing Studios.

"The first track we recorded was 'Diamond Rings' and the rest is history."

"We wrote ['Diamond Rings'] and I thought nothing of it. Naughty Boy sent it off to Chipmunk, who really liked it and wrote his stuff around it." The track would go on to be a major hit for Chipmunk and Emeli's first taste of chart success when it was released in the summer of 2009. Emeli and Naughty Boy's collaboration had only just begun.

The duo followed up the song 'Diamond Rings' with three more tracks that would lead to future hits. They wrote 'Daddy' – a song that would provide Emeli with her second solo hit – on a car journey from Luton Airport to Ealing, during which Naughty Boy played Emeli a beat he had come up with in his shed. To his astonishment, she improvised the rest of the song there and then. The songs 'Mountains' and 'Clown' followed soon after. Both artists quickly realised there was no method to their songwriting; it seemed to come naturally, which perhaps explains why Emeli has become such a prolific songwriter for other artists, as well as proving successful in her own right. "I feel like I'm always writing songs," she said. "It's my purest form of expression I think, because I was shy growing up and I used to put everything into songs."

"We would have a conversation and it would take off from there," Naughty Boy said. "It was that natural. Those were the first songs we wrote. We didn't know what was going to happen when we wrote those songs. We liked listening to them, but we didn't have proper management or any proper guidance. Certain songs like 'Daddy' and 'Clown' reflected the place we were in back then. We didn't know if we were going to have success or be able to carry on. We didn't have a studio and we didn't have any money. I'd spent all my *Deal Or No Deal* by 2009 on my shed and I'd spent two years trying to hone my craft and make music, so we were both broke. Until I met Emeli I wasn't confident enough to work with real artists and singers. I felt I wasn't good enough. As great as Emeli is, working with her built up my confidence."

"It was a real struggle," Emeli said, "it was us against the world, it felt like. No one really believed in us and nobody was that interested in what we were doing. But we kept going and we really had faith."

Throughout this period, during which the duo nurtured their talent and self-esteem, they held back from trying to set up meetings with publishers and record labels, for fear of rejection. But when 'Diamond Rings' became a hit for Chipmunk, reaching number 6 in the UK charts in the summer of 2009, the major airplay and sales brought the music business to their door.

"There was no management on the scene at that time,' Naughty Boy said. "Adrian, who is now Emeli's manager, was around. But there was nothing official. When 'Diamond Rings' became a hit and was getting played on the radio we had no official management and we had no publisher. So it was nice to get played on the radio, because people found out about us through that song."

But despite the initial flush of success created by 'Diamond Rings', the rejection the Scottish singer so feared was just around the corner – and it would come from a surprising source.

In 2009, Universal Music Group gifted Take That's Gary Barlow his own record label, Future, in return for his masterminding Take That's successful comeback.

Formed in 1989, the five-piece vocal group had become Britain's most successful boy band and released the two bestselling albums of the decade before they split in 1996. Ten years later, minus Robbie Williams, four members reunited and found themselves enjoying another phenomenal spell of success. When Williams rejoined them for their sixth studio album, 2010's *Progress*, it became the fastest selling UK album of the 21st century and Barlow's Future Records was already under way.

On launching the new imprint, Barlow announced he was looking for new and exciting young talent. His first signing was English classical artist Camilla Kerslake. Other signings followed, including Brazilian rapper Aggro Santos and Scots singer-songwriter Emma's Imagination, both of whom enjoyed short-lived success in the UK charts.

Barlow also invited Emeli to audition for him in a piano room at the label's headquarters in London. But after she performed one song, Barlow said he didn't think she had what it took to be a star. Emeli had chosen to sing 'Clown', which at that moment summed up her feelings to a tee: "I guess it's funnier from where you're standing/Cause from over here I missed the joke/Clear the way for my crash landing/I've done it again/Another number for your notes". She left the audition in tears, aware she had a stark choice ahead: she could accept Barlow's apparent expert knowledge as gospel and forget about a career as a solo artist or she could keep going and prove him wrong. But Naughty Boy knew she was made of stronger stuff, and he made a mental note of the event, feeling that somewhere along the line Emeli would succeed despite what Barlow said.

In fairness to Gary Barlow, he wasn't the only one who couldn't see the Scottish singer's star potential. Back in July 2009, she was struggling to convince the music business at large that she could cut it as a solo artist. Patience and patients were needed in big supply, since she also had to balance her efforts to make it in the music biz with her neuroscience degree studies back in Glasgow.

Emeli's manager, Adrian Sykes, recalls this period in her life: "Her work ethic was remarkable. Monday to Thursday, she would be walking the wards and attending lectures and doing what young trainee doctors do. Then she would fly down to London on Thursday night and be in the studio until Sunday night. She'd fly back up to Glasgow on Monday morning, get on a white coat, put the stethoscope around her neck and start all over again. She worked incredibly hard. It all comes down to having the right work ethic, instilled in her by her parents."

At the time Chipmunk's 'Diamond Rings', which featured Emeli's vocals on the chorus, was receiving major airplay on Radio 1 after DJ Jo Whiley picked it out as her Pet Sound and the station's Weekend Anthem. "It's just strange that some little song I wrote in my bedroom got us so much success and airplay. In fact, it's crazy," said Emeli of the experience.

The week before the release of 'Diamond Rings', Emeli gave one of her earliest newspaper interviews to the *Daily Record* after a performance at Glasgow's legendary King Tut's Wah Wah Hut. "The song 'Diamond Rings' is a metaphor for anything good you've done recently or anything that's made you feel good about yourself. It gives you that swagger, you feel important because of it," she explained.

She also gave a rare insight into her transition from niche soul singer to pop star in the making. "My flatmate, May, has known me since I was eight, we grew up together," Emeli said. "She was there when I did my first little song on the piano and is used to me doing jazz stuff and more soulful songs. So when I ask her opinion on a pop song I've written she always says it's wrong and I have to explain that I need to please people and can't keep it to myself and my little niche crowd. I can still relate to a Joni [Mitchell] song, even though it's 25 years old. That's the main and important thing to me. I'm not too bothered about what category my music goes in. But I don't want it to be too cool for school. There's no point in limiting who you can reach. But I want it to be respected. I have different influences for the different aspects of what I do. For piano playing I just look to someone like Nina Simone, for songwriting I love people like Tori Amos and Regina Spector. When it comes to singing it has to be Lauryn Hill – I can't get enough of her voice. But when I was growing up I loved Mariah Carey, I still love her. I am a diehard fan. When it comes down to it, it's Mariah always."

That night at King Tut's, few were there to see the singer with the wide smile and big hair. She was, after all, supporting the Californian-born but London-based Natty, a popular reggae star whose single 'July' had been a club favourite the previous summer. But when Emeli opened her mouth to sing, the room was silenced before the crowd finally erupted into spontaneous applause. Just a week later, a whole new audience would be captivated by the Scottish singer with the big voice.

On July 5, 2009, Chipmunk released 'Diamond Rings', the third single from his debut studio album, *I Am Chipmunk*. The song peaked at number six in the UK Singles Chart and brought Emeli to the widest audience yet. But she missed her chance to capitalise on the song's success; her studies kept her from starring in the promo video set in a Prohibition-era speakeasy, and a model was drafted in as a miming replacement.

In August, *The Sunday Times* twigged that the "beautiful cabaret singer who combines twenties glamour with an incredible soul voice" featured in the video was not all she seemed. "Sandé, though young, lovely and voluptuous, is no twenties flapper," the *Sunday Times* wrote. However, anyone who has seen Francis Ford Coppola's 1984 movie classic *The Cotton Club*, a crime drama centred on a thirties Harlem jazz club of the same name, will know that Emeli could have fitted into the video's Roaring Twenties staging without any trouble. She was already exuding a style and charisma in keeping with classic blues and soul artists, such as Nina Simone and Aretha Franklin. And while many would think the music industry had drafted in a more suitable face for the flapper role, the real reason for Emeli's absence was that she was sitting a statistics exam on the day of the shoot. At 22, she still had two years of her medicine degree to complete and had just passed an intercalated degree in neurology with flying colours.

"It was annoying but these things happen," Emeli said of the missed opportunity. "But I did really well in the exams, so it was worth not being in the video for that."

Another opportunity that never was came in the form of a polite ban from the university's annual medic talent show. Having won the contest two years in a row, the university asked her not to take part for a third time. "I don't blame them really," Emeli said. "The plan is to sign a record contract later in the year, write songs and build an album, and when I graduate to hit the ground running."

Finishing her education was one of the most important things to Emeli, whose manager, Adrian Sykes, had been patiently fostering her music career since she was 16. "Adrian respected that I wanted to get an education. My parents were keen that I finish university. It was really good having people behind me who weren't rushing me to do something or didn't respect what I was trying to achieve. I managed to pass my exams in medicine and make things happen in music."

Diane Sandé believes that her daughter's decision to put her education at the heart of her career ambitions indicates her strength of character. "No matter how much faith you have in your child, the music industry is so difficult," she explained. "People say things are going to happen and then things change. The fact that she chose to go and do her degree showed a lot of maturity. She didn't place all her eggs in one basket. She was sensible enough to get her university degree and decided it would be important and valuable."

Emeli credits her parents and their struggle to create the best life they could for their daughters as being key to her tremendous work ethic. "My dad is a very focused man. He has a very great mind actually. He was one of the cleverest people in his country, then he came to England.

'He always made it clear to me that education is very important, and that you have a responsibility to achieve something and make something of your life. And that was very important to my mum as well. They were both the first people in their families to go to university and they never hid any kind of struggles from my sister and I. We were never wrapped up or protected from any of the realities of life. We both knew what we had to do."

Now, having abandoned her first name, Adele, and adopted her middle name, something amazing was happening. Emeli would soon take the steps that would lead her down the same path as the other Adele, and become one of the hottest British soul singers of her generation. Still, she continued to hedge her bets: would it be a career in medicine or music? The decision was now upon her. Should she put on hold her musical ambitions to pursue her studies full-time, or give up singing altogether?

Fortunately, further encouragement was just around the corner.

By August of that year, the word that Emeli would be the Next Big Thing in music was spreading fast and Scotland's national newspaper, the *Daily Record*, reported that the medical student from Alford had signed a publishing deal with EMI Music. Not to be confused with a record deal, which concerns itself with recordings that are released to the public for purchase on CD or digital and other formats, along with revenue from airplay on broadcast media, a publishing deal relates to revenue generated by an artist's songwriting. Songwriters compose songs for artists from behind the scenes – they never break their cover, yet their best compositions can become major hits for some of the biggest name stars in the business. Perhaps from EMI's point of view, Emeli's Top 10 hit with Chipmunk and string of songwriting collaborations with other artists was enough to merit her signing. If so, the label must have been delighted when, down the line, she became a major artist in her own right.

The publishing deal came just as Emeli was about to start her fourth year at the University of Glasgow. A joyful Emeli, just 22, told her friends: "I am now a professional songwriter." A record deal allowing her to record those songs, however, was still a long way off.

Behind the scenes Emeli was still working hard to be recognised not just as a songwriter but as a performer in her own right. The chance to shine came at an event that was right up her street.

Having just completed her third-year exams, Emeli heard that 'Diamond Rings' had been nominated for Best Song and Best Music Video at 2009's MOBO Awards and that she would join Chipmunk on stage during the performance of the hit song. Her songs were finally getting the recognition they deserved. "I have been working towards this since I was 11 and, 11 years later, here I am," she said. And 'Diamond Rings' wasn't a one-off – as well as providing Chipmunk with his first Top 10 hit, Emeli had also written a track for Girls Aloud's Cheryl Cole, who recorded Emeli's 'Boys' as the B-side to her chart-topping single '3 Words', the second single from her debut solo album of the same name.

The success of 'Diamond Rings', her collaboration with other artists including Cheryl Cole and the publishing deal should have given Emeli all the confidence she needed to go full out to cement her status as an artist in her own right. But past encounters with the music industry had made her all too aware of the battle she faced to convince labels she could go it alone. A year before, Adele Adkins had broken the mould by showing that female chart stars didn't have to be stick-thin pop puppets or scantily clad catwalk wannabes to succeed, when her debut album, *19*, topped the charts. But Adele remained the exception to the rule, and the vast majority of the British female crop of singers being groomed for the charts in 2009 still measured up to the old stereotype. Still, she had a platform for her voice: the time was now.

"The collaboration with Chipmunk was the one that made her realise that perhaps she shouldn't wait and keep away from music for another year," John Ansdell, the Glaswegian who first signed Emeli after discovering her on Gumtree, recalled. "She said 'Maybe I should go for it now', and she did."

Emeli decided to take a year out of her medical degree, which quickly paid dividends. She no longer had to turn down the chance to perform or engage in songwriting assignments because she had to be in class or in a hospital ward. Finally, she was able to get down to the business of making music. With the ink still wet on her publishing contract with EMI, Emily could now look forward to growing her profile at the upcoming MOBOs and persuading labels to take her performing as seriously as her songwriting. And some record labels were already starting to take notice.

"I went to London to do showcases for about six different record companies," she said, acknowledging that several labels had been interested in signing her up. "But I wanted to be in a stronger position, so that's why we considered releasing a single independently."

The independent release would be 'Daddy'. If she could make a success of an independent release, she'd finally be able to prove she could make it on her own.

Her parents, meanwhile, waited patiently, in hopes that good news would soon come. Diane said: "She must have been wondering what was happening. She was writing songs for other people and record labels saw her as a writer rather than an artist in her own right. She is grounded enough that she coped with that and didn't get desperately anxious about it. Even as a child, she was very calm and not one to jump up and down for attention."

One reason for Emeli's initial struggle to secure a record deal was that she had become a victim of her own success as a songwriter. "I built a reputation as a songwriter in the industry before my own hits. People were used to coming to me for songs. There were songs like 'Clown' and 'Mountains' that were my songs that I wanted to keep. But the record labels saw me as a songwriter. It was hard to get people to believe in me as an artist. The song 'Clown' was written when I couldn't find anyone who believed in me as an artist. Maybe those labels will think twice next time a young songwriter comes along."

Well aware that there was an upside to the music industry ignoring her, she said at the time: "As I'm doing so much writing, I'm building up a stack of songs – so far I have three songs that I would definitely put on an album, so I just need seven more."

With a growing collection of songs and a renewed faith in her talents, Emeli decided to take the plunge and moved to London. Finally, she had the chance to go full throttle on a music career that was revving up nicely. The move also plunged her smack-bang into the middle of a thriving urban music scene, a far cry from the feeling of isolation she experienced growing up in a small town in Scotland and being mixed race.

"I moved to Scotland when I was four," she said. "We were the only black people there. That was very isolating. It made me feel I needed something, and that's where music came in. It became my world and where I could connect with people. It was just, you were just different. You were like an alien. I didn't suffer any racism, but I just felt very different. Was it in my mind? No. You want to know how to do your hair, you want to know how to fit in. You want to feel part of something and meet people who like the same kind of music. So, as soon as I could, I headed to London."

However, ironically, the urban music scene was moving to Scotland. In fact, it was heading straight for Emeli's old stamping ground, Glasgow.

For the first time in MOBOs history, the awards show was to be held outside England's capital city, at the Scottish Exhibition and Conference Centre (SECC). As the ceremony drew closer, there were reports that relocating it from London to Glasgow would prove a damp squib. Under the headline 'MOBOs or Maybes', the *Daily Mail* asked: "As Scotland prepares to host a top music awards ceremony, why are all the big stars so keen to stay away and leave it to the lesser talents?"

The article continued in the same vein: "Beyoncé and Jay Z are unlikely to attend. As is Dizzee Rascal. Leona Lewis is not even nominated this year, but it is hoped that Alesha Dixon will be there. On paper, the MOBO Awards 2009 – blazing a trail north to Glasgow for the first time next Wednesday – should have the makings of quite a spectacle. It is a line-up that screams bling, that promises the sparkliest dresses, the longest limos, the baddest, sharpest bodyguards, the whitest trainers, the tightest rhythms. Or it would be a spectacle if any of the real big hitters of MOBO – music of black origin – could find space in their busy schedules to turn up. As it is, the biggest American name among those confirmed to appear in Glasgow on September 30 is Jermaine Jackson – and he is not nominated for anything. He will be there simply to front a special tribute to his late brother Michael."

But the newspaper should have known that Glaswegians are renowned for being able to throw a party. On September 30, it really was a star-studded affair as guests arrived by private jet, limo, helicopter and Harley Davidson motorbikes to the event being broadcast live on BBC3. On stage, Jermaine was joined by sister La Toya to pay tribute to their sibling Michael Jackson, who had died just three months earlier in controversial circumstances. Their version of 'Smile', which saw them joined on stage by *Britain's Got Talent*'s street-dance group Diversity and teen singer Shaheen Jafargholi, was a moving climax to the awards. Boy band JLS and hip pop group N-Dubz took home two MOBO awards each, while Chipmunk beat international acts Eminem and Kanye West to win the Best Hip Hop Act gong. As such, the night was also a triumph for Emeli.

While Emeli was getting a kick out of the success of her first chart single and Top 10 hit, across the Atlantic a musician was getting a spanking from the record label that released the track. 'Diamond Rings' sampled 'Miss Ska-Culation' by Roland Al & the Soul Brothers, but it was a Canadian artist who found himself on the wrong end of the lawsuit.

John O'Regan is a musician best known by his stage name Diamond Rings. In December 2009 he released 'All Yr Songs', but the video for the track was removed from YouTube at the behest of SonyBMG on the grounds of copyright infringement. At first the Ontario singer couldn't understand why the promo had been pulled. The controversy went viral and SonyBMG, realising that it had slipped up, withdrew the claim against O'Regan and issued him and the video's director, Colin Medley, with a formal apology.

Copyright hiccups aside, the song was to be the first of many hits involving Emeli and Naughty Boy. And despite the success of a single that could easily have been mistaken for another 'bling' track, Emeli had no intention of letting the chart placing go to her head. Not for her the desire to quaff champagne or be seen on the red carpet at the opening of envelopes. "I think the hip hop scene in the UK isn't about money and extravagance," she said. "It's a bit more astute than that. You can't be talking about all this money if you don't have it. That's what makes it interesting, talking about things people can relate to."

Almost nine months after Chipmunk took the track to number six, the pair enjoyed another chart success. And yet again for Emeli, it was as a featured artist. On February 28, 2010, the single 'Never Be Your Woman' was released by Relentless Records (a subsidiary of Virgin), billed under the artist name Naughty Boy Presents Wiley feat. Emeli Sandé. Describing it as a tough grime anthem for veteran rapper Wiley, one London newspaper critic wrote: "New London soul girl Emeli Sandé also boosts her rep." The track, featuring a sample of White Town's nineties dance number one 'Your Woman', became a Top 10 hit. It was enough to land Emeli her long-awaited recording contract.

"I tried to bang down a lot of doors, but Virgin were the only label who believed in what I was doing," Emeli recalled. "I ended up with the label that understood what I was trying to do."

Emeli's perseverance had paid off. As 'Never Be Your Woman' climbed to number 14 in the charts, she could finally announce to the world that she had landed a record deal. First she called her mum and dad, in Alford, and her sister, Lucy, in London, with the news that a celebration was in order. "I'm signed," she said. "I'm an official recording artist with Virgin Records."

6. TEARS IN 'HEAVEN'

In quantitative terms, Emeli had done three-quarters of a six-year degree in medicine before deciding to take time out, but she refused to rule out going back. But Naughty Boy had already been there, bought the T-shirt. In fact, he'd gone one better by dropping out of a university degree in Business, Marketing and Music altogether. He needn't have worried that his parents would be disappointed in him if he didn't succeed in the music business. Recalling the degree course, he said: "It wasn't creative enough. They were asking me too many scientific questions. By the time the other students had graduated from that course, I'd had a Top 10 with Emeli, so I had graduated as well, though without a degree."

But both were still tentative about signing to a major label. "Me and Emeli both signed to Virgin Records," he said. "I signed first then Emeli signed. Before that people were interested. There is something I want to address. I have never addressed this. But I feel that it is right to. The labels weren't sure. There was other label interest and a lot was happening. But we didn't know where we stood."

However, Virgin's decision to sign both Emeli and Naughty Boy would prove to be astute. In fact, Naughty Boy has since gone on to experience his own chart success with his 2012 debut single, 'Wonder', his chart-topping single 'La La La' and his 2013 album,

Hotel Cabana (with Emily featuring on eight of the album's tracks, including 'Wonder').

But for John Ansdell, who had been trying to get funding for a deal and had come so close to signing arguably the biggest British female artist of the decade, it was a cruel blow. Though delighted for his protégé, he had narrowly missed out on going down in history as the man who signed Emeli Sandé. "I ended up getting the funding I had been trying to get for a year," Ansdell said. "It was unfortunate that [it] came through just as she got her Virgin EMI record deal."

With a record deal now firmly under her belt, it was time for Emeli to get down to writing her album, and she wanted Naughty Boy to remain a part of the magic formula. And he was glad to be involved. "With Emeli's album I could get my teeth into something. From 'Heaven' to 'Clown', the songs we wrote, the intention was to say something." Though some songs were written, others were still being handed over to a plethora of other artists desperate for quality material. In fact, one of those artists was signed to the label that had rejected Emeli just a few years earlier: Gary Barlow's Future Records.

Aminata Kabba was born and brought up in Freetown, Sierra Leone, but her family fled as civil war raged and her mother's hairdressing salon was bombed. The Kabbas moved to London where a teenaged Aminata, who changed her identity to A★M★E, proved to be a style conscious and talented young singer and, in 2011, she was signed to Barlow's label. When the label went bust, she landed on her feet with a UK number one hit in April 2013, featuring on Duke Dumont's 'Need U (100%)'.

By then, Emeli had already banked an impressive number of co writes with both unknown and famous artists, and she would also team up with the teenage singer on one particular song, although the pair never met. Instead, A★M★E headed into the studio with Naughty Boy to work on a song idea of Emeli's called 'Find A Boy'.

"It was a track I wrote with Emeli and Naughty Boy," A★M★E said. "Not a bad thing to have on your resumé, definitely not. Emeli had written, I think, a verse and a chorus but she wasn't there when I went into the studio with Naughty Boy. We worked on the song some more and I recorded it at his studio."

For her own album, Emeli decided to take a different tack. She and Naughty Boy decided to go cold turkey on the pop charts altogether, which allowed them to become immersed in their own creations and come up with their original sound.

As Naughty Boy recalled, "When we were writing the album, we weren't listening to the radio. We wanted to make music that said something. It is hard to change things in the music game. A lot of music is daytime radio and you're always up against that in your head. It is easy to worry about whether it will be radio friendly, but all that went out the window. We just wrote some amazing songs and hoped for the best."

According to Naughty Boy, the new deal turned out to be a perfect fit. Virgin gave both him and Emeli the freedom to develop tracks without the pressure to meet sales targets. It is an all-too-common mistake for labels to try to cash in on the latest trend, only for their artists to miss the boat or bomb with a substandard copycat style. Quite apart from the fact that Emeli wouldn't have put up with such a scenario, thankfully the label stayed out of the picture, confident its investment was a sound one. "There wasn't any pressure from the label making the album," he said. "It wasn't like Emeli was a big star or that there was any anticipation. We didn't know what it was going to do at all, and I love that."

During this period Emeli and Naughty Boy would collaborate with Tinie Tempah on the track 'Let Go'. UK hip hop artist Tempah had spent 11 months perfecting his debut album, *Disc-Overy*. A mixture of grime, drum and bass, R&B and pop, it featured collaborating artists on the album including Ellie Goulding, Kelly Rowland, Swedish House Mafia, Labrinth and, of course, Emeli.

By October 2010, Tempah – real name Patrick Chukwuemeka Okogwu Jr – was champing at the bit. He'd been building up some serious steam since 2005, with the release of several mix tapes and various independent tracks. Building his audience from the ground up, he was finally signed to a label after an audacious move saw him run a competition on his blog, in which he invited the winning label – Parlophone – to celebrate the deal with high tea at Claridge's. The following year, he released the singles 'Pass Out' and 'Frisky'. When it came time to release a third, 'Written In The Stars', Tempah revealed his frustration at having to sit back as other urban stars cleaned up in the charts and at awards shows.

"When I was 16, I had a huge underground hit and I was travelling out of London doing gigs for a couple of hundred quid. That was major. Life couldn't be better. People knew who I was and I was having fun. I got caught in that bubble. I started to doubt things when my peers made the transition to popular culture and landed major record deals and I hadn't. I started to feel envious and jealous and began resenting people and music. I was angry at myself for a long time because it had happened to everybody else, people like Chipmunk, Tinchy Stryder and N-Dubz, who are friends of mine. But it hadn't happened to me. I wished it was me."

The distant past needn't have concerned him – his debut single, 'Pass Out', had stormed to number one and would become the biggest-selling single of the year, launching Tempah into the stratosphere – but it made for a good rags to riches story. He added: "When it started to happen for those people, I was like, whoa, what happened to me? I felt left behind and there were times when I thought it wasn't worthwhile. But I stuck at it and tried to make it happen. I feel everything happened at the time it did for a particular reason. There were a few dark times on the way up, but those points are necessary in one's career to make you ready for the journey ahead."

Articulate, stylish and intelligent, Tempah's career tale had paralleled Emeli's. Both had worked hard in search of recognition. Both had kept their dignity and both were finally seeing their hard work pay off. As 'Written In The Stars' battled for the top spot in the British singles chart with 'Let The Sun Shine' by pal Labrinth, Tempah spoke of the pride he felt for his debut album, which was due for release in a matter of days, and of his admiration for Emeli, who featured on *Disc-Overy*. By now, Emeli had moved lock, stock and barrel to London and the year out from her studies looked increasingly likely to be extended, perhaps permanently. As Tempah's album shot straight to number one that weekend, having sold 115,000 copies in just seven days and pushed Labrinth (who had produced 'Written In The Stars') into the number two spot, the hip hop artist from Plumstead predicted big things for the Scottish singer.

"She is incredible," he said. "She is one of the most talented vocalists we have in Britain. She has an amazing voice. She has a doctorate. Having her on my track was incredible. She has a song called 'Heaven', which I cannot stop playing. She is amazing and I am honoured to work with her. She definitely is the future. That's an inside tip."

Emeli was similarly effusive about her counterpart. "Tinie has influenced a lot of people who don't listen to hip hop. Tinie is a great guy. It was great working with him. He is really humble and a cool guy."

And Tinie Tempah's tip proved, indeed, to be a hot one. In fact, Emeli's career was starting to generate some serious heat. But she continued to pay her dues the old-school way, playing gigs no matter how small. Of course, some of those smaller gigs are a rite of passage for any band.

Such was the case with her return to Glasgow's King Tut's in November of that year. The venue, which has a capacity of just 300, is situated on Glasgow's St Vincent Street and has won numerous awards including best UK venue. Having opened its doors in February 1990, King Tut's is also famous as being the place at which Glaswegian Alan McGee, then boss of Creation Records, spotted an unknown band called Oasis and signed them on the spot. Artists such as the Strokes, Coldplay, Franz Ferdinand, Blur, Radiohead, Pet Shop Boys and Primal Scream have all taken to its tiny stage. But Emeli was about to prove she could hold her own among such legendary company. Playing as part of a mini-Scottish tour, backed by a four-piece band, she opened with the song 'Kill The Boy' and killed it. If the atmosphere seemed muted, it was because the audience were savouring her soulful voice. When she introduced the new song 'Ready', a spontaneous roar of applause broke out followed by an almost karaoke-like atmosphere that greeted her climactic mash-up of her collaborations with Wiley, Chipmunk and Tinie Tempah. To finish, Emeli mesmerised fans with her now famous track 'Daddy' – and found herself being forced back onstage to chants of "One more tune!". For many new artists, it is a struggle to provide additional material in the event of an encore. But it was no such problem for Emily, who had been storing up songs for years, many of which would become tracks on her debut album. And she didn't disappoint, ending the homecoming gig with an unrehearsed, yet spine-tingling, version of 'Clown'.

By late 2010, Emeli had also featured on British rapper Professor Green's 'Kids That Love To Dance' from his debut album, *Alive Till I'm Dead*, and admitted: "Everything is snowballing. I am really happy. I have just recorded a session with Magnetic Man and my own album is coming out next year. The first single released in February. … I have just finished a track with Devlin.** We are all coming up at the same time so it is exciting. Everyone is really excited. I love the team at Virgin. They really let me be creative and bring my ideas."

There was clearly a mutual respect among those artists who had worked hard to break through from the underground scene to hit the mainstream. Some sort of critical mass appeared to have brought urban music to the fore, and it was even more welcome for the creativity attached to it. The songs had swagger, bite and style, and Emeli seemed to have become a litmus test and a common denominator. If she was involved, well, it had to be good. By now she had drawn the

---

** *Bud, Sweat And Beers*, the debut studio album from underground MC and hip hop artist Devlin, featured Emeli on the track 'Dreamer'.

attention of *X Factor* boss and Syco label chief Simon Cowell, who described Emeli as "his favourite songwriter at the minute".

Perhaps the path to stardom would have been that much easier were Emeli to have auditioned for the show – after all, Simon clearly liked her. But she had already decided long before that the TV talent show wasn't for her. "People would always ask 'When are you going to go on *X Factor*?' I think [I didn't do it] because since I was seven or eight I wanted to be a writer and it was so important to me that I would sing and deliver my own songs. I'm a songwriter and want to be in full control of what I do ... That was the only reason holding me back. I just wanted to take a bit of a longer and harder route and really learn how to write a song."

However, Emeli believed there were positives to such talent shows: "I like that *X Factor* gives people a platform. A lot of people who have won it would never have had a chance of getting signed by labels. I can see the good and the bad of *X Factor*. If it works for someone, they should go for it. I never thought about that, even though it took me so long to get recognition. It never crossed my mind to go on it."

Always on the search for new talent, Cowell has never been one to miss out on star potential; no matter that Emeli never auditioned for one of his shows – he had other ideas for her.

The English music mogul has enjoyed an illustrious 30-plus years in the music industry, ever since his dad secured him his first job in the record industry back in 1980. He grafted through various positions and helped indie label Fanfare enjoy several hit singles, including with their first signing Sinitta, who became a star when her second single, 'So Macho', sold 500,000 copies on its third release, in 1986. Cowell's role in bringing a variety of mainly pop acts to the public's attention during the next couple of decades is well documented: Curiosity Killed the Cat, Sonia, Robson & Jerome, and Westlife were among them. He is also famous for unleashing novelty acts on an unsuspecting public, including children's TV characters the Teletubbies and *Big Breakfast* puppets Zig and Zag.

Emeli Sandé performs at Glasgow's Oran Mor in 2010. PKIMAGE

Emeli with classmates at Alford Primary School in Aberdeenshire. As a pupil, Emeli took recorder and ocarina lessons and it wasn't long before teachers at the school realised she had a talent for singing too. WENN

With sister Lucy and mum and dad Joel and Diane during a candid moment at home. WENN

The first of many red carpets as Emile arrives for the MOBO awards in Glasgow, on September 30, 2009.
ANDY BUCHANAN/AFP/GETTY IMAGES

Emeli enjoys a catch up with mum Diane and dad Joel as she visits her old school, Alford Academy, in August, 2011.
HEMEDIA/SWNS GROUP

Now a pop star in her own right, Emeli holds a Q&A session with pupils at Alford Academy and performs her songs 'Next To Me' and 'Clown' to the delight of the children and teachers. HEMEDIA/SWNS GROUP

Emeli performs at the Belladrum Tartan Heart Festival at the Belladrum Estate, near Beauly, Inverness-shire, on August 6, 2011.
SCOTT CAMPBELL/REDFERNS

Emeli and Professor Green attend the MOBO Awards at the SECC on October 5, 2011 in Glasgow, where the pair perform the song 'Read All About It'. SANDY YOUNG/GETTY IMAGES

Emeli, Chipmunk and Wretch 32 at the Raymond Weil Pre Brit Awards Dinner hosted by Labrinth at Mosaica, The Chocolate Factory on January 26, 2012, in London.
DAVE M. BENETT/GETTY IMAGES

Emeli at a Biz Session to promote her new album *Our Version Of Events* on July 13, 2011, in London.
DAVE HOGAN/GETTY IMAGES

Singer Jessie J presents the 2012 BRITS Critics Choice award to Emeli during the nominations announcement for the BRIT Awards 2012 at The Savoy Hotel on January 12, 2012, in London. DAVE M. BENETT/GETTY IMAGES

Emeli wins the innovation award, presented to her by Tinie Tempah, at the Nordoff Robbins O2 Silver Clef Awards on June 29, 2012, in London. DAVE M. BENETT/GETTY IMAGES

mile performing at Lovebox festival in London's Victoria Park, on June 16, 2012. DARRAN ARMSTRONG/CORBIS

As well as numerous songwriting collaborations, recording sessions and live performances, Emeli's breakthrough would require numerous photo shoots such as this one on November 22, 2011. DIANA GOMEZ/CORBIS OUTLINE

He would later capitalise on the mass market appeal of the television talent show, establishing the multi-billon pound franchises *Pop Idol*, *The X Factor* and *Britain's Got Talent*, all of which have spawned multiple versions across the world, and become a major star in his own right for his no-nonsense critique of the acts auditioning on his shows. His success is so impressive that few would begrudge him his status as one of Britain's most knowledgeable music impresarios.

Who knows quite when Emeli was brought to his attention. Perhaps he had been keeping an eye on her for some time, but one thing is certain: he was fully aware of her talent when he lined up a songwriting assignment for her alongside another of his greatest successes, the winner of 2006's UK *X Factor*, Leona Lewis.

Lewis had turned to Emeli for help on the follow-up to her chart-topping 2009 album, *Echo*. Emeli said: "I'm meeting with Leona soon to go over four songs I've written which could go on her new album. It would be amazing if she decides to use any."

The fact that *Echo* had been executive produced by both Cowell himself and the legendary Clive 'The Music Man' Davis – former President of Columbia Records, former Chairman and CEO of RCA Music Group and a star maker to a cast of protégés that reads like a *Who's Who* of the music industry – should have been a clue that Emeli's career was heading down the right path. These guys are no slouches. If Emeli was good enough for them, she was good enough for anybody. And she was proving she was up to the hype; by now, other songwriting credits were coming to light – for Pixie Lott, the Saturdays and Alesha Dixon. There was talk of her working with Susan Boyle, or Su-Bo, as the Scottish singer and runner-up sensation of the third series of *Britain's Got Talent* is affectionately known. But the public would have to wait for the results of the Lewis recording sessions, by which time Emeli's own solo career would be gathering pace, and then some.

Meanwhile, Emeli carried on gigging. In June 2011, she got her first real taste of the festival circuit when she played RockNess music festival, near Dores, Inverness-shire. By that point Emeli had topped the UK album charts as well as enjoyed two Top 10 singles, albeit as a collaborator, and was making a name for herself as a major songwriter. Now she was excited for the chance to show what she could do on her own.

Emeli had every right to feel at home as she performed at the festival, the location of which is, in relative terms, a stone's throw from her home in Alford. The annual music weekender, launched in 2006 when dance star DJ Fatboy Slim took his Brighton Beach party to the banks of Loch Ness, is certainly one of the most picturesque events of its kind in Europe, and Emeli was delighted to be included on the bill. "I come from a little village called Alford in Aberdeenshire," she explained during STV's digital coverage of the event. "My dad still teaches at the Academy and my mum works in Aberdeen. They think it is very exciting. My mum keeps me updated if anyone mentions me or if there are any clippings in the local newspapers."

Emeli giggled when I met her in the artists' village that overcast afternoon as she prepared to make her festival debut on the Rock'N'Roll Circus stage. Relaxed in front of the film crew, she seemed to be taking the upcoming launch of her solo career in her stride. It was a sign that her confidence was growing, which she acknowledged. "In the past couple of years I have been able to hone my craft, and working for other people has taught me a lot about writing songs," she smiled. "Featuring on other artists' work has taught me a lot about the business, so now it's my turn."

As she prepared to unleash herself upon the RockNess crowd, Emeli also revealed she had pretty much finished her debut album: "There is a song called 'Heaven', which looks like it will be the first single. The songs 'Maybe' and 'Daddy' are there. I know they're going on the album. We finished writing a month ago and started recording last week. The musicians are amazing and I'm really happy with how it's sounding. It bridges that gap between the urban world and the songwriting I do for other people. I'm excited about introducing myself this way. It's a good feeling to have experience. It is also quite daunting not to be the featured act, but it's exciting."

For the time being, though, she was also excited about playing to a crowd that would include some familiar faces. "I'm really looking forward to the atmosphere at RockNess and playing my songs. I'm very excited, also because it is in Scotland. All my friends and family are going to come along."

Many of the acts performing at music festivals say it's a chance for them to catch other acts of whom they themselves are fans, and Emeli was no different when asked about her experience of RockNess. "It's not as glamorous as Aberdeen," she joked. "No, it's amazing. It's really nice to be back in the countryside. I used to camp close to here so it is nice to be back. I've seen Ms Dynamite. I loved her. She is amazing. I remember when her album came out. It was one of the first things I had heard from Britain of a female bringing stuff out that was speaking to me, and her lyrics were really well thought out. It's amazing to come and see her now. We've worked together as well now. It's really brilliant. It's starting to rain but everyone is having fun."

Sharing the bill with rockers Kasabian, dance duo Chemical Brothers and Glasgow rockers Glasvegas, as well as another Scots singer, Paolo Nutini, who would headline the main stage in front of the biggest crowd in the festival's history, Emeli added: "This is my first time so I'm just going to experiment and see what happens. The best thing is to get up there and do your thing and see how they react and then fine-tune it for the next time."

And she'd need to keep at it, as she acknowledged she still had some way to go to make herself stand out from the crowd. Despite changing her stage name from Adele to Emeli some years before, Miss Sandé had yet to escape the comparisons with the 'Rolling In The Deep' singer. However, she admitted to being flattered. "It's great. I'm a big fan of hers. We are very different lyrically, but it's flattering to be compared to her because she is really good. She stands out because her lyrics are so honest and a lot of people can relate to them."

Everything seemed to be coming together for Emeli. But despite her successes and a debut album in the making, she hadn't yet ruled out a return to Glasgow to complete her degree in neuroscience. Speaking several months prior to the RockNess appearance, she revealed she was yet to decide between medicine and music. "I came to Glasgow to study medicine for five years," she explained. "I'm on my year out. I still have 18 months in which to finish off the course. I want to go back and do that. It'll be hard, but I just want to finish what I started. We'll see. This time next year things could be really different."

It would be another eight months before Emeli's album *Our Version Of Events* was released, but within days of her performance at RockNess she was to support one of her musical heroes. "On Monday, I'm supporting Alicia Keys at the Royal Albert Hall, which is the dream gig of my life," she revealed. As a child, Emeli had loved to sing along to Alicia Keys' songs at her piano in her living room. Now she would be supporting her idol on the big stage.

The atmosphere inside the Royal Albert Hall was electric. Before taking to the stage, Emeli admitted: "I'm really nervous, but at the same time I'm super-excited. Alicia Keys has been so inspirational to me and my music."

As Emeli performed, it became clear she had amassed a body of material that must have been the envy of many chart stars. Afterwards, she commented on her dream gig: "To play the Royal Albert Hall was insane and to support Alicia Keys on the 10th anniversary of her album *Songs In A Minor* was amazing. I used to listen to it all the time when I was 14. It was crazy to get that slot, I loved it. To have people around the world knowing your songs like that would be incredible. I didn't get to meet her, sadly. I met everyone but her – her husband, her manager, but not her."

But the disappointment of not meeting the soul and R&B superstar would abate; soon after the Albert Hall show, Emeli would be sitting at a grand piano in a New York studio, writing songs with her idol. She would go on to form a friendship with the soul singer from Hell's Kitchen, New York, which would lead to her making inroads into the US music industry.

The album, however, was still some way off and perhaps it was this that led Emeli to tell the *Daily Record*: "We've been writing forever now. We're good to go with the mixing and mastering." Emeli had enlisted top producer Jim Abbiss to work on her debut, and she was in good company; Abbiss' previous work included hit albums from Adele, KT Tunstall and Noisettes. It was only a matter of time until Emeli would join them in their chart success.

For now, it was festival season, and another appearance came in August of that year at the Belladrum Tartan Heart festival. The slot was in the middle of the afternoon in the Hothouse tent, but come showtime the tent was barely half full. People milled around on the fringes and outside, enjoying spells of sunshine. Emeli's debut single, 'Heaven', was due out in a matter of days, yet hardly anyone at Belladrum seemed to have a clue who she was. Instead, they appeared to have wandered in for shelter or out of curiosity. Mothers parked their buggies and dug out snacks for their toddlers and babies.

Situated near Beauly, Inverness-shire, the picturesque Belladrum estate has held the family-friendly festival on its grounds for the last decade. The two-day festival sells out quickly and has a capacity of just over 15,000. Children are entitled to free entry with parents and the vibe is as far removed from the behemoth rock weekenders Glastonbury or T in the Park as it is possible to imagine. If Glastonbury is hardcore, Belladrum is softcore. Children laze in hammocks in the sun, Black Isle ale, champagne and Pimm's are served up to revellers determined to kick back and let themselves be impressed by whichever act happens to be on next. With an eclectic mix of entertainment, it's not unusual to find people wandering around the beautiful Belladrum estate with its walled gardens, savouring the beauty of the landscape with the music as a backdrop.

That year, Emeli shared the bill with Deacon Blue, Texas, Echo & the Bunnymen, Kassidy and chart stars Anna Calvi, Newton Faulkner and Ed Sheeran. It was 2.30 p.m. The Hothouse tent may not have been packed to the rafters, but anyone concerned with Emeli's ability to win over the audience needn't have worried. As soon as she began her set, which included soon-to-be-household-favourites 'Heaven' and 'Daddy', everyone stopped what they were doing and took note. As Emeli gripped the microphone, her rolled-up sleeves revealed a tattoo of the Mexican artist Frida Kahlo, which runs the length of her right forearm.

Emeli would have been forgiven for worrying that the mediocre attendance would be reflected in sales of her debut solo single. But if she was nervous, she didn't intend to show it. "I'm really excited about it," she said of the impending release. "It's getting played all the time on Radio 1, which is amazing. I remember the first time I heard it on there; it was 2 a.m. and I was coming home from the studio and I heard it in a taxi. It was really cool. I wrote 'Heaven' about five months ago with Naughty Boy. ... The song came really quickly and had a life of its own. We just knew it was a really special song."

Yet having featured on so many other artists' albums, she had resisted the temptation to call in favours as she planned her own debut. "So far there are no collaborations but we will see. Maybe something will happen over the next couple of weeks."

But although she accepted that there was an added responsibility to bringing out an album in your own right, she revealed she was ready for it. "I guess there is more pressure because I'm not hiding behind anyone and this is my campaign – but it's nice to introduce myself properly and say 'this is just me'. It always was the plan to do my own thing. Even in the beginning before working with anyone. It was just a case of finding the right time, feeling like I was ready and having the right songs."

Except Emeli wasn't truly alone. She had the moral support of her friends and family, who were still the first to hear her new songs as they came together.

"It is really nice to hear [them]," mum, Diane, said. "She and Lucy are in London, but when she was here, you could tell when she was developing a song. You could hear the song growing. It's fantastic. I still remember hearing 'River' and 'Clown' from the album for the very first time. I would play the songs and I would record them onto a CD and play them in the car. They still bring a tear to my eye."

Dad, Joel, added: "Every time we heard the songs we knew they were really good, but it was hard to tell if they would be commercial. We were the first to hear the songs on the album."

Emeli also revealed she had the full support of future husband Adam Gouraguine. "Adam may be a marine biologist but he appreciates music and loves listening to my stuff, and if I've written a little song, I'll always show him first. But he's not musical; I've tried to teach him piano a few times but he got really impatient. I had to leave that one." Yet Adam had helped her career in other ways: "I've done a few shows in Montenegro [Adam's home country] and he's been my translator," she said. "I wouldn't expect my music to be appreciated over there but they just love jazz and there's such a crowd for that sort of thing. I couldn't speak their language but I can communicate through music. It was really cool."

As the plaudits from all over Europe started to flood in, Emeli continued writing songs for other artists. Enjoying the fresh Highland air at Belladrum, she revealed. "I have just finished a song with Cher Lloyd, called 'Lifetime', for her new album. I have ... one that has been recorded by Susan Boyle. That's probably my proudest moment. Susan recorded my song, called 'This Will Be The Year', last week, for her next album. She's an amazing character and an incredible artist. Scotland's got a lot of great artists and we support one another. It's good to wave the flag. There's another called 'River', which I'm hoping she's going to record. I've sent the songs over and I'm looking forward to hearing what they sound like. I haven't met her yet. I just sent her the song. I'd love to meet her because I think she is a bit of a rock star."

Emeli also revealed that the collaboration with Leona Lewis, engineered by Simon Cowell, had yielded fantastic results. "I have songs on Leona's album. She'd heard a couple of songs, so we had a week in the studio with her. Then we had another week together.

It was very natural. Leona and I got along really well. She recorded a song called 'Trouble' and another called 'Mountains', so I look forward to hearing them on her album."

And there was more: "I've also got a second single coming out with Professor Green called 'Read All About It'. He is lovely and great to work with. There are lots of people I'd love to work with – like Nicki Minaj, and Robyn: she's an amazing artist."

Emeli, meanwhile, had songs of her own to get busy with if she was ever going to get her debut album released. "I'll maybe write another few songs and see how that goes but I'm really happy with how the album is sounding. 'Heaven' is one side of it but every song is completely different," she said. "Lyrically, yes, I guess it is typical but every song will have a different life of its own. 'Heaven' is getting on all the playlists and I'm really happy. It's on the A-list at Radio 1, which is amazing."

Support from a local station had also proved important in the weeks leading up to the release of 'Heaven'. Gary Muircroft had arrived at Northsound 1, the number one radio station serving Aberdeenshire and North East Scotland, weeks before Emeli was due to release her first solo single. Now the Content Director for Northsound, Tay and MFR, Muircroft had been appointed Northsound's Programme Director and on hearing that Emeli was from his patch, he decided the station ought to champion this local talent.

Muircroft takes up the story: "There wasn't much awareness in the station of Emeli Sandé. It was very low. The record plugger got in touch and as soon as I found out she was from Alford, we looked at it completely differently because the north-east is such a small area. It is only 300,000 people. We heard 'Heaven' and also got to hear the planned follow-up singles. I thought she was fantastic. But you never know, and it's great to see her reach the heights that she has. Back then we bought into Emeli's 'Heaven' song before most, largely because she was from Alford. It was pre-release of the single that she came to the studios for the first time. She was introduced to Greigsy who does our breakfast show."

Greigsy (full name Greig Easton) was happy to chat to the local girl, but didn't consider himself to be sitting in front of the next UK superstar. "She had been to T in the Park and had just been signed to Virgin EMI when she came in on a Monday morning to do the show. Her promo team were just about to do a radio tour, but they thought they'd try her home station first. This innocent girl who didn't look like a pop star at all. There was nothing outstanding about her. She was a real normal looking girl and she had a very normal style. We get the Saturdays in and they are glammed up to the max. They are styled and sexy and tight and revealing. Emeli just rolled in as if she was out for lunch. She was very casual and didn't shine like a pop star. I remember she was incredibly shy. The first single, 'Heaven', was a few months away. We played it and had a wee chat with her. We were hoping for big things for her but we never thought this girl was going to go as global as she did, not initially. It wasn't until later when we got to hear some of the album that we started to think, God, this girl could actually do something."

Muircroft said: "All we did was support the single as a radio station and we probably played it more than most because she was in our area. It was a bit of a gamble in the beginning to go so heavy with it, but it started to take off pretty quickly across the UK. The song became massive."

Muircroft and Northsound 1's support had a knock-on effect across Bauer's network of independent radio stations as they all followed suit, first B-listing the song then A-listing it ahead of release. "All the Bauer stations work closely together. With her getting on the Northsound B-list then moving on to the A-list ... it would have made a difference," Muircroft said. "It's a great song and it's down to the talent first and foremost. There was an appetite for the song."

Emeli's links to Glasgow also gave her the local edge at another Bauer station, Clyde 1 FM, which serves Glasgow and West Central Scotland. "Aberdeen was her home for many years and that's why we supported ['Heaven'], and Clyde supported it because she had studied in Glasgow," Muircroft explained. "The two radio stations felt close to her. Once you have the backing of the two biggest radio stations in Scotland, obviously stations like Radio Forth and Radio Tay were going to support it as well."

It wasn't long before Muircroft had invited Emeli along to Northsound's studios to take part in their charity Cash for Kids lunch, held at Aberdeen's five-star Marcliffe Hotel. "Prior to the single becoming so big we had booked Emeli for a Cash for Kids ball – before it had even hit the charts. Emeli came along with her family." Emeli performed the track in front of the 150 guests. "They saw her before she had huge success with that single," Muircroft said. "She was very focused on getting well known in her local area. That meant a lot to her. Because she had studied at Alford Academy and her dad works there and her mum worked in the city of Aberdeen, I think it was really important to her. She has never forgotten her local area and I don't think she ever will."

Leading up to the release date, 'Heaven' topped the Shazam chart, which is based on millions of daily requests for songs played on the radio, and in bars and clubs. Emeli said at the time: "It has been number one on Shazam for weeks. People just want to know what it is they are hearing, which is really exciting."

Two weeks later, in August 2011, Emeli achieved her dream and released her long-awaited debut solo single. And all of the groundwork Emeli had put in immediately paid off. Radio 1 DJ Fearne Cotton made 'Heaven' her record of the week after the station A-listed it. The reviews were mainly positive. The youth culture magazine *i-D*, founded in 1980 by former *Vogue* art director Terry Jones, remains faithful to the street-style roots of the early *Vogue* editions, and is cutting-edge when it comes to youth, fashion, art and music. The magazine wrote of the Scottish singer: "Emeli Sandé is not the next so and so; she's the person other acts will be compared to in the coming years."

Virgin Records was keen to get the message across, too. The press release that accompanied the single stated: "Not many people know it, but Emeli Sandé was behind some of the biggest tracks of

2010. Now she's about to be the voice and songwriting talent in front of the freshest debut single of 2011. As someone who sweats the art of songwriting as much as the singing, she knows it's about being contemporary and timeless. 'Heaven' is both those things, a euphoric feel-good summer track packed with lavish strings, bombastic horns and trip hop beats all combined with Emeli's subtle yet soaring vocal. With her shaved head and Frida Kahlo tattoo, the 24-year-old Aberdonian chart star has collaborated with some of the greatest names in modern pop and scored two Top 10 hits: grime Godfather, Wiley's, 'Never Be Your Woman' and Chipmunk's 'Diamond Rings', which she also co-wrote. A piano player since the age of 11, the multi-instrumentalist's revered writing talents and incredible voice have also led to her co-writing/featuring on tracks with Tinie Tempah ('Let Go'), Professor Green ('Kids That Love To Dance') and Tinchy Stryder ('Let It Rain'). Richly melodic, classically powerful and retro-futurist, the deferred medical student's (specialising in neurology) own songs are as interesting and as individualistic as she is. Her intuitive intelligence, self awareness, and empowered honesty is hugely apparent in her lyrics." Waxing lyrical, the release continued. "Emeli's love for and understanding of artists like Nina Simone, Joni Mitchell, Roberta Flack and Lauryn Hill are obvious, loud and proud."

Emeli admitted: "[The press release] was my idea. I had to really push to get people to change their perception of who I was, because when you establish yourself as a writer it's hard to get people to see the other side of what I do. It was a push, but I'm glad it worked."

Now she faced a short and nervous wait to see if her bid for solo stardom would yield results. Emeli said: "I'd signed as an artist a year after I'd signed my publishing contract. It is quite a nerve-racking time when you're about to release the first solo single, because I knew I loved it but you never know how people will react. There was no longer a rapper to front the thing and I couldn't hide in the chorus any more. This was fully my expression and my vision, I guess, so putting it out there felt very liberating but at the same time quite a daunting thing. When the radio started to play it and people began to have an interest in what I was doing it was incredible."

Among those willing Emeli on to steal the top spot was her labelmate Kylie Minogue, who used Twitter to voice her support and, once again, it spurred the idea of another collaboration.

"I can't get my head round the fact that Kylie tweeted me," Emeli said. "It's a bit crazy. It would be fun to do something with her later down the line."

With the benefit of airplay on the Beeb's youth music station and independent radio stations up and down the country, as well as the following Emeli had built up as a result of constant touring and guest spots, 'Heaven' looked like it was on course for the number one spot. But despite all the support, and with sales of 63,659 in the first week, the song stalled at number two, narrowly losing out to Wretch 32's 'Don't Go'. Emeli wasn't complaining. "It charted at number two and that was the beginning of the *Our Version Of Events* journey."

Now enjoying fame as an artist in her own right, Emeli admitted to *The Sun*'s showbiz editor Gordon Smart that she was struggling to get used to being recognised. "Getting my picture taken is a bit awkward," she told him. "It's really strange when people recognise me on the street. I'm trying to get used to it but it's a bit odd."

For Emeli, now a bona fide solo star, it was time to take stock. But she had no intention of slowing down. "I'm writing all the time," she said. "I do feel a bit weird if I'm not writing, and I'm always trying to get to a piano. I just write about things I'm experiencing and feeling, and that is usually inspiration enough. Also people's stories around me, things from family and friends – but usually it's just what I'm experiencing, growing up and learning. It was maybe a bit different but it was nice to grow up in Alford, there were no distractions: I had to study or write songs. I just wanted something a bit bigger. Now I'm in London and it's really exciting for me, but I'm really glad I had that background to help me develop my craft and understand what I'm doing. I don't get the chance to get home that often. It is very calming, I think I should go home more often."

Emeli now looked forward to the day when she could return to her old school, Alford Academy, to perform for the students. "I've felt really embraced by people, especially other artists. It's like people are supporting real music," she said. "My music teacher is really excited for me, so I'm looking forward to going back and seeing everyone."

At this point, Emeli believed her album would be released before the year was out, but in the end she would have to wait until February 2012 before it was made available. She also had the release of Professor Green's 'Read All About It' to look forward to. Emeli said: "It was weird for me to sing a song I hadn't written, but I found vocally I was able to bring something to the table."

Green had penned the song as an angry response to claims made by his stepmum, Jackie, that he had cashed in on his father's death after Peter Manderson was found hanged in 2008. The urban star – real name Stephen Paul Manderson – planned to perform the song with Emeli a week before its release, at that year's MOBOs at Glasgow's SECC. "The song is close to me," he said. "There have been a few things I didn't get to say to my father before he passed so it was a scary one to put it there in the song. It is probably my most open song to date. Emeli is incredible. There is a mutual respect as artists but we get on as well. She has a fantastic voice, her writing is incredible and she doesn't look bad either. She is the whole package. I don't think anyone else could have conveyed that emotion on the song. We work really well together." He also let slip that his second album, *At Your Inconvenience*, would include the song 'Astronaut', co-written with Emeli.

Ahead of the upcoming MOBO Awards, Emeli's credibility would get another boost when she secured one of music's most sought after TV spots, on the BBC's *Later... with Jools Holland*.

Former Squeeze keyboard player Holland has fronted the music show that has become an institution and favourite of British music lovers for 20 years. First aired on the BBC in 1992, its fans adore it because it concentrates almost entirely on the music its guests play with the exception of a short chat between Jools and one of that week's guests, often followed by him accompanying said artist on piano. Past performers read as a *Who's Who* of music greats, from Leonard Cohen and Johnny Cash and June Carter Cash, to Oasis, Al Green and David Bowie, to name a few. When Emeli appeared on the BBC 2 show on September 23, 2011, alongside indie heavyweights Snow Patrol and folk-rock veteran Roy Harper, it was proof positive that she was considered a class act.

'Read All About It' was gathering plenty of airplay by the time Glasgow's MOBO Awards came round again. The awards ceremony, founded by Kanya King in 1996, is chiefly designed to honour and promote music with a connection to British black culture. Since Emeli's dad was Zambian and her repertoire had been inspired by some of the greatest black artists of all time, she was a shoo-in to perform. But there was another pleasant surprise. She was also nominated in the Best Newcomer category alongside Ed Sheeran, Wretch 32, Jessie J, Rizzle Kicks, Jamie Woon, Yasmin, Alex Clare, Loick Essien and Maverick Sabre.

She had Ms Dynamite's vote.

The half-Scottish, half-Jamaican singer, who was born Niomi Arleen McLean-Daley, knew a little bit about what makes an award-winning recording artist, having won BRIT, Mercury Music Prize and MOBO awards in her own illustrious career. She had also featured on a string of other people's hit songs as well as enjoying recognition in her own right, beginning with Sticky's 2001 underground hit 'Booo!' right up to her Mercury Music Prize-winning album, *A Little Deeper*, just a year later. "I've been listening to Scottish R&B and soul singer Emeli Sandé, who I love," she told *The Independent*'s Charlotte Cripps.

At the MOBO Awards, South London's Dionne Bromfield sang a tribute to her late godmother, Amy Winehouse. Those in attendance on the night – including boy band JLS, who got a ringside seat – watched in awe as Emeli shone during the performance of 'Read All About It' with Professor Green. Emeli, who in the end lost out on the MOBO to Jessie J, was thrilled by the response to the performance.

But not half as thrilled as she was during a private moment in her dressing room because behind the scenes, Emeli was given the sort of surprise that even a glittering awards ceremony can't beat. Her boyfriend, Adam, proposed to her and Emeli, taking a deep breath, said 'Yes'.

It was the finale to an amazing year for Emeli: she'd finally shown she could stand out as a solo star, she was one of the most sought after songwriters in the industry, and now she had a future with Adam to look forward to. But there was one thing she'd have to let go of: "I realise I'm probably not going to be a doctor now. ... A lot of my friends who are junior doctors now say that the hours are hardcore. I still keep in touch with them as much as I can because they work crazy hours and I am down here, but they visit when they can. I always have extreme choices to make. I thought maybe I could enjoy this and just make music a hobby, but then it got to a point where I thought I really need to try this now and make a go of it."

And make a go of it she did.

When 'Read All About it' was released that October, the first play had come just weeks before when presenter MistaJam debuted the song on BBC Radio 1Xtra. However, it was Professor Green and Emeli's live appearance on October 23 on the *X Factor Results* show which guaranteed the song would be a hit. Not only was the track "a smash", as radio DJs of old would have called it, but 'Read All About It' went straight to the top of the charts.

One man could be proud of his contribution to helping Emeli become a star, or rather he would have been, had he not forgotten about her. When Emeli and Professor Green appeared on BBC Radio 1Xtra's *Live Lounge*, fronted by Trevor Nelson, to promote 'Read All About It', Emeli reminded the embarrassed veteran DJ that he'd given her her big break as a 16-year-old. At the time, Nelson had only recently been honoured at the Sony Radio Academy Awards with a Lifetime Achievement award for his services to broadcasting, so he can easily laugh about the fact that he failed to appreciate his part in Emeli's story. He said: "She had taken part in a talent contest for a show I did, but I didn't know. Everybody was always telling me about how this girl Emeli Sandé was incredible. I thought 'Who is this girl, Emeli Sandé?' I completely forgot she had done the talent show years ago on [*The Lowdown*]. She had changed her name and it didn't ring a bell.

"Before I got her in to do a session for me at Maida Vale with Professor Green, I was speaking to Professor Green down an ISDN line and I got her in the background. I said to Emeli 'I really got to meet you'. She said, 'Yeah, yeah'. She came into the studio a couple of weeks later and did an interview with me. The first thing she said was, 'You don't remember me, do you?' and then she reminded me of the story and it was probably the single most embarrassing moment I have ever experienced on radio ... in a nice way."

Nelson is another key figure in the music industry who not only appreciates Emeli's talent, but the fact that she has established herself on her own terms. "Emeli's career has gone beyond what anyone could imagine. She could have any career that she wants because she has got it on her own terms. I do seven shows a week across three BBC networks yet I can play Emeli Sandé on all of them. Musically, she has got that incredible range that transcends all ages."

By now described by critics as a Scottish superstar-in-waiting, Emeli had sold out a London date in hours ahead of her first headline tour. The concert on November 7, 2011 was one of a string of intimate sell-out dates that included shows at Glasgow's Òran Mór – the same venue at which Emeli had showcased as an unknown – and Edinburgh's Caves, both still a far cry from some of the giant performances still to come.

On November 10, she joined Tinie Tempah onstage at Wembley Arena, alongside another guest, former Destiny's Child singer Kelly Rowland. Earlier that same evening she had played the EMI *New Music Sessions* at London's Abbey Road Studios. As soon as that gig was done, she hailed a cab to Wembley. Things were happening fast. She said: "I couldn't miss a chance like this. I haven't even had a chance to tell my mum I'm playing Wembley. She's going to kill me."

Although Wembley was a massive deal, perhaps Emeli's most special gig during this time was at Howford Primary School in Glasgow, where she met children benefiting from the work of the Nordoff Robbins music therapy charity. The late Paul Nordoff was an American composer and music therapist who developed the Nordoff Robbins style of music therapy with the late Dr Clive Robbins in 1959. Run by musicians and managers from across the British music industry, the charity continues to work with people of all ages by providing music therapy to transform their lives. That night, journalist Maggie Barry was there to cover the visit, which ran in the *Sunday Mail* under the headline 'MOBOs... X Factor... Howford Primary'. Barry recalls: "Emeli was great with the children, who have special needs. She was amazed when a little 11-year-old boy, Rahul Mehemi, stood inches from her and sang every word of the song 'Heaven' back to her. I don't think she could quite believe it."

Emeli said: "It's very moving to see how powerful music can be and it was really special to see how using music can activate different skills. It was very simple yet incredibly effective. The kids were amazing and it was astonishing to see just how the music gets to them straight away."

Gordon Duncan, the Scot who has helped coordinate Emeli's publicity campaign since before the release of her debut single, said of the rising star's appearance: "The fact that she is really into the Nordoff Robbins charity and has followed her association through, visited one of the schools and given a music therapy class and staged a benefit concert, is a sign that she wants to use her success to help when she can, particularly when it is causes close to her."

Other gigs that month included the BRMB (now Free Radio Birmingham) Live concert in Birmingham alongside JLS, James Morrison, the Wanted, Cher Lloyd, Pixie Lott, Matt Cardle and Tinchy Stryder. "She looked a little lost on the vast black stage, but debut single 'Heaven' tingled the spine," wrote the *Sunday Mercury*'s Graham Young.

And as the month drew to a close, Emeli was to release her second single from her upcoming debut album. According to those involved, Emeli was the one who pushed for the release of 'Daddy' as her next solo single, though many of her team regarded her stint as a featured artist on Professor Green's 'Read All About It' as the release which would consolidate her chart status. But, despite not making it into the Top 10, 'Daddy' was still considered a chart success, if less impressive than her debut offering. And since the release date for the album had been put back to early 2012, it helped maintain her public profile. The single also generated glowing reviews in the press. The influential Digital Spy website gave it five stars, as did the *Daily Record*, while *The Star* gave it nine out of 10. The fact that the critics were firmly behind her gave Emeli added confidence as she continued to work round the clock to establish herself in the UK. She wouldn't have much longer to wait.

With the year drawing to a close, Emeli found herself the recipient of Best Breakthrough Artist at the 13th annual Tartan Clef Awards, while Scottish radio station Northsound 1 continued to champion the singer. An example of the support her local radio station bestowed upon its favourite daughter came when mid-morning presenter John Mellis recorded a special Christmas broadcast dedicated to the rising star, calling the show 'Emeli Sandé: Our Version Of Events'. Her debut single, 'Heaven', had reached number two in the national charts, she had enjoyed a number one collaboration with Professor Green, completed her own mini-tour and, by now, had supported Coldplay – arguably one of the biggest live bands in the world – on their European tour. "I've just come off tour, then a radio tour then here," she told the *Daily Record*'s showbiz reporter, Bev Lyons, of her growing schedule. "Coldplay kicks off next and I'm very excited, but I need to get some rest first." Outside of the coveted support slot, she had plenty more to look forward to, not least her debut album being due for release in February. In December 2011, the rest of the world was just starting to take notice of the young singer from Alford, and Mellis and Gary Muircroft wanted to make sure the north-east of

Scotland was up to speed on the most talented singer-songwriter to come out of the area since Annie Lennox. Mellis introduced special guest Emeli as having gone from being nobody to being number one, from playing in the cold to supporting Coldplay, from meeting her idol to being idolised.

During the in-depth interview, Emeli gave a clue to the secret of her success when Mellis asked her to advise others hoping to follow the same path. "I would say instead of chasing companies the best thing I found was just focus on your music and be very critical with yourself and to really think about the sound that you want and present it as a whole sound, and present yourself when you are really confident about what you want to do." She also revealed her uncompromising nature when it came to the artistic process. "I think some people get so caught up in trying to get signed and trying to impress and trying to please and bending themselves to whatever these companies want that they kind of get lost. You're never going to have a long career if you do it that way. So I'd say learn your craft, get confident with what you are doing, gig a lot and they'll come to you. If it's great, they'll come."

Confessing that things were looking very positive ahead of the album release, she added: "I haven't released my album. I haven't done anything like that, but it feels good and it feels like I am establishing myself as an artist."

As well as describing the inner drive that had helped her to make it this far, Emeli had more words of encouragement for listeners wanting to emulate her growing success. "If you do work hard at something and you really want it, then it's easy to achieve if you keep going, no matter how many knock-backs," she said. "Just because it is a tiny town in the middle of Scotland, don't think that we can't achieve what we really want. Just go for what you want."

The presenter's relaxed style of interview teased out some little-known facts about the fledgling superstar, not least that she was shy and introverted offstage, too shy even to call the stars she had written hits for and suggest going out. "There's a few people I can add on the phone, but I don't feel cool enough to hang out with everyone, so I just keep to myself."

However, it was the quiet aspects of her personality that had led her to express her feelings through song in the first place. "I was very shy growing up. I guess that's why I got so involved in music. I really enjoy being onstage. I really enjoy delivering the songs and getting that electric feeling. You are risking everything onstage so I love that, and there are certain songs I feel like I know exactly how that song should be delivered. It's one of the reasons why sometimes I'll think I need to keep this song for me."

No doubt, Emeli was receiving the kind of cumulative exposure most new artists can only dream of. By now, it was also becoming clear that she could appeal to a broad spectrum of music fans, from the young girls eager to catch a glimpse of JLS star Aston Merrygold's abs to those more interested in Chris Martin's cerebral coffee-table rock music.

Yet there was still work to be done.

Jessie J stole the limelight at the Capital FM Jingle Bell Ball in the run-up to Christmas, with Emeli barely mentioned in the press reports. But her days of being ignored would soon be over and other artists were taking note.

English rapper and singer-songwriter Example, real name Elliot John Gleave, had enjoyed one of the year's biggest hits when 'Changed The Way You Kissed Me' shot to number one. "I met Emeli very briefly at the Q Awards, although I should have come into contact with her a lot more. She has worked with a lot of my mates in the scene. Ed Sheeran told me she is amazing and he thinks her album is better than Adele's. I pay quite a lot of attention to him."

Sheeran had also played the Belladrum Tartan Heart festival, where he raved about the album tracks that Emeli had played him long before they were released. "She let me hear the tracks. They're incredible. I think she can be bigger than Adele's album," he said with a twinkle in his eye that suggested he meant it, though it seemed like a bold statement at the time, since Adele was on course to sell four million copies of her second album, *21*. Yet his prediction may turn out to be true. At the time of writing, Emeli has sold over four million copies of *Our Version Of Events* worldwide and she has barely scratched the surface of the American market. Still, Emeli couldn't rely on the plaudits of her peers to steer her debut to the top. Before the album's release, Emeli plugged away in the run-up to Christmas with her gruelling live schedule, heading to venues like Dublin's Sugar Club.

But shortly before that promotional whirlwind Emeli discovered she had been nominated for the BRITs Critics' Choice award, alongside Maverick Sabre and Michael Kiwanuka. Ironically, had Emeli persuaded labels to back her years before, she would not have been up for the career-defining award, since the criteria stipulates that nominees can have released singles, but they must not have released an album's worth of material. Fortunately, her original 'album' release with John Ansdell – snapped up by those 300 or so people who attended her launch at Glasgow's Òran Mór two years earlier – didn't count, since it had never really been commercially available. Now those years of struggling to get noticed were paying off and because she hadn't rushed into a solo career, she looked a very likely winner.

With her second single, 'Daddy', being lined up for a release date to coincide with the BRIT Awards as well as the release of the album, it was surely too much to expect all the stars to align for this remarkable, yet modest, Scot. But at just 23 years of age, she was now on the verge of becoming a recipient of the same award won by Adele in 2008, Florence & the Machine in 2009, Ellie Goulding in 2010 and Jessie J in 2011. All had gone on to enjoy huge fame and both mass and critical success, but Emeli had to wait another week before the winner would be announced. If anybody was curious as to how she was feeling about the nod, then the song 'Clown' pretty much summed it up.

"When I look back, I was writing 'Clown' about it being hard to get a deal, finding it hard to find people in the industry who were interested in me," she said. "There's a line: 'I guess it's funnier from where you're standing because from over here I'm just a joke.' People always laugh at you when you're trying to be creative or achieve something and putting yourself out there, so it's me saying I'm prepared to be the clown."

After years of writing for others, Emeli could stand proud in her own right, whether or not she would go on to win the award. "It was never a struggle as a songwriter because I think I was doing something that no one else was," she said. "People were always interested in my songs, just not me as an artist. I don't think we're in an industry where people take risks, or at least we weren't when I was trying to get signed. But things are changing now and people are looking for something different."

The timing of Emeli's nomination could not have been better. If she went on to win, she could reasonably expect to collect the accolade around the release date of her debut album, in February 2012. What better publicity for launching her first collection of songs? Once again, Emeli had every right to be hopeful. Normally reluctant to tempt fate, she admitted: "I've been really blown away by reactions and feel so confident. I'm really happy about being nominated. If it was anything else I'd be like, 'OK, may the best man win', but I want it so much. I remember when Jessie won last year. I was sitting at the BRITs thinking 'wow'. Now it could be me."

Around this time, Emeli also got the news that she would be performing 'Read All About It' with Professor Green on the hour-long Christmas Day special of the legendary chart show *Top Of The Pops*. She would be joined by Pixie Lott, the Wanted, Example and 2011's *X Factor* winners Little Mix. Emeli said of the opportunity: "It's a great honour to perform on the show that I watched growing up in Aberdeen."

TOTP presenters and Radio 1 DJs Fearne Cotton and Reggie Yates made no bones about their admiration for Emeli during their introduction to the performance: "She is a singer of such grace and humility and deserves our adulation."

Despite her increasing profile and reputation, not all of Emeli's collaborations saw the light of day. Barbadian outfit Cover Drive – best known for their cheeky anthem 'Lick Ya Down' – revealed they had worked with Emeli before she became famous, but chose not to use her material after she met them in a recording studio for a songwriting session. Cover Drive's singer and main songwriter, Amanda Reifer, said: "Emeli Sandé was the writer on one of our first writing sessions in London. She did mention to us that she was not signed at the time, but what is for you, you will get and it was always for her. We wrote a song together, but didn't use the song for the album because, although it was a feel-good song, it didn't suit us as a band. But I can't tell you the name of it because it may end up being sung by someone else and that wouldn't be fair. She's an amazing talent with an incredible voice. We're so happy for all her success."

Despite missing out on earlier opportunities, Emeli was taking full advantage of her illustrious support slot on the Coldplay tour. As the tour was coming to an end, she reflected on what it had meant to her to support one of the biggest British bands of the last several decades. "[It] went really well and was enjoyable, a lot of fun. I have been loving playing arenas but I love it when I strip it back – to the lyrics and voice. I learned a lot from how [Coldplay] operate. They looked professional and I was well looked after on the tour, and it was a chance for me to introduce myself to people all over Europe, in big arenas holding as many as 17,000 people."

Back home, matters of a more personal nature awaited. That Christmas, Emeli and her boyfriend of seven years, Adam Gouraguine, told her parents they wanted to get married. Joel Sandé was thrilled, though his sense of humour was as dry as dust as he recalled the moment Adam broached the subject. "It was nice when Adam came to ask for permission for Adele's hand in marriage," Joel said. "Obviously, permission was granted."

Meanwhile, with Christmas just 10 days away, Emeli got the news she had longed for. She was still on tour with Coldplay in Europe when she discovered she had won the BRITs Critics' Choice award. Uniquely, in terms of BRIT awards, the recipient of the Critics' Choice award is notified that they have won months in advance of the ceremony taking place. "When I found out I had been nominated I was on Christmas holiday in Montenegro with my fiancé. Then I went on to win it," she said. "It was an incredible feeling. It was amazing. I was backstage in Paris on the Coldplay tour when I found out and I was running around screaming, as you would. I've dreamed of winning a BRIT award since I was young. Things have happened so fast. What does it mean to win the BRITs Critics' Choice? … It was incredible because I had been at the BRITs before. Nobody knew who I was. But I remember watching Jessie J receive the award and thinking how amazing it would be to receive something like that."

With the ceremony, which would take place at the O2 Arena in London in February 2012, still a couple of months away, one of the first people to praise Emeli for her win was her Critics' Choice predecessor. "I'm so proud and happy for Emeli Sandé for winning," Jessie J enthused moments after the announcement. "Congratulations girl. Here's to 2012 being your year."

As it turned out, even Jessie J – who had experienced what a Critics' Choice win at the BRITs can do for your career – could not have imagined just how much 2012 would be Emeli's year. And by now Emeli was well aware that she had to put every waking moment into establishing herself as an artist in the hearts and minds of the public. Manager Adrian Sykes says that Emeli never complained during this time. Quietly, she went about the business of turning up at the 4 a.m. photo shoots and late-night recording sessions. She smiled for TV and radio interviewers, was humble during phoners, face-to-face chats with the press and those endless live performances. There were no days off and very little sleep, but she never complained about being tired. Throughout it all, Emeli had a professionalism that impressed everybody she met in the business. This included Tom Odell, who by remarkable coincidence, was recording his debut album next door to Naughty Boy's Ealing studio; a remarkable coincidence because the year after Emeli triumphed with her BRITs Critics' Choice win, she would present Odell with the same award. Himself a young hopeful when he first heard Emeli trying out her new songs with Naughty Boy, Odell recalls the time he first heard Emeli: "I was aware of Emeli because she was on the radio tons. I actually had a studio next to her at one point where she was making her album so I was aware of her before she got big. When I first moved up to London just after I signed my record deal I got Sony to rent me this tiny little writing room ... I'd go there and write songs all day and Emeli's records would be leaking through the wall. It's quite funny; when I met her at the BRITs when she gave me the Critics' Choice award we were talking about the mad world that you can be next to each other. I'd never actually met her but it's mad that she won the Critics' Choice as well and we had a studio next door to each other."

With the nervous wait to launch her solo career now a thing of the past, Emeli kept busy as the BRIT Awards ceremony loomed. "I have been doing a lot of writing for other artists and trying to finish off my own recording," she said. Thrilled to be collecting a BRIT award and looking ahead to the event itself, Emeli said: "I'm over the moon at winning a BRIT. It hasn't quite sunk in yet. I am just very excited and my family are all excited for me. I can't wait to be at the BRITs. ... It's been an amazing year. It was the perfect Christmas present to hear that I had won it."

Now a bona fide star, Emeli had to get an image to match. Some time beforehand Emeli had ditched her afro and dyed her hair a striking white blonde. Even more daring, she debuted a hairstyle which would become her trademark: a stacked mountain of hair up top, with a close-shave on the rest of her head; in other words, a very modern-day mohawk. But despite the dramatic image change, she was still laid-back when it came to styling. "My tour manager is a woman and my hairstylist is a woman, so they are my female company when I'm on the road. I'm a last-minute planner so I will pick something to wear a few days before the BRITS. Last year was definitely about Adele's performance and seeing her all stripped back. I remember watching the BRITs as a kid. It's such a glamorous event. I just remember when I was younger and thinking how amazing it would be to be involved."

When the bells rang to mark the passing of one year into another and 2012 showed its face, Emeli had plenty of reasons to feel optimistic. As one of Britain's hottest rising stars, she now had her pick of homegrown artists for collaborations. Now Emeli, who was preparing to perform at the BRIT Awards 2012 Nominations launch party that January, had another collaboration in mind. She wanted to team up with the best America had to offer after a successful songwriting partnership with Alicia Keys, and she was not so much aiming for the stars as the superstars: Motown legend Stevie Wonder and queen of R&B Beyoncé were on her radar.

Emeli said: "I've had a few people requesting songs but everyone assumes that I am pretty busy at the moment. There are lots of people I would like to work with, so hopefully I can clear some time. The biggest thrill would be to work with someone like Stevie Wonder – if I could write a song for him it would be a dream come true. I'd love to continue working with Alicia and I'd love to work for Nicki Minaj. That would be incredible. I'd love to work with Beyoncé. Her voice is unparalleled. She can do anything with her voice and it is a great pleasure when you work with someone that shows their voice so well."

Still the comparisons with another stellar vocalist persisted. "Adele is a great writer and has an incredible voice," Emeli said. "I love to tell stories with my music and I think, from what I've heard of Adele, she does the same thing, so there are similarities there. But we have written in different styles. I can't wait to release my first album, so that everyone can hear the full story of what I do. That is the one thing I am really that excited about – the release of the album. It is pretty much finished and I think people will hear a different side, maybe something they haven't expected if they have only heard

'Heaven' and 'Daddy' and the track with Professor Green. It is a very musical and very honest record and I am proud of that. My background comes from songwriting on the piano and people might not be expecting that if all they have heard of me is 'Heaven'. There will be moments on the album that are a lot more intimate and a lot more stripped back. The title *Our Version Of Events* came out when I was having breakfast with Naughty Boy, the producer, and my A&R guy. I think it is the perfect title."

January 2012 also brought the news that Emeli had teamed up with the Sugababes to help them with their comeback album, but the announcement was understandably overshadowed by the nominations launch. Stage and TV actor James Corden introduced the star-studded event at London's Savoy Hotel on January 13. Twenty-year-old Suffolk singer-songwriter Ed Sheeran led the nominations list with four, ahead of Adele and Jessie J who were both up for three. Florence & the Machine and Coldplay were also up for a pair each, as were Bon Iver and Aloe Blacc in international categories. Emeli was hotly tipped to add to her Critics' Choice award and take home the gong for British Breakthrough Act, despite competing against Jessie J, Sheeran, Anna Calvi and the Vaccines. No wonder Emeli was smiling as she took to the stage. She had gone public on her engagement to long-term boyfriend, Adam, and she was on the verge of releasing the debut album she had been dreaming up for years.

Two weeks before the official album release, Emeli was back in Aberdeen, performing at Northsound 1. "We were lucky enough to get the official press launch party for *Our Version Of Events*," Greigsy said. "She launched it in the north-east of Scotland. She did it in her home city. She came along and did an acoustic set. That was the first time I had heard her sing live with a live audience. It was amazing. I was blown away by her to be honest. It was just her, acoustic guitar and a keyboard player and 40 invited listeners. Everyone was mesmerised as she did her three or four songs. She did it at the studios here in the live lounge area. We streamed it live if I remember right. She was incredible."

On February 11, just moments before she was due to take the stage at Heaven in London, and two days before the album's release, Emeli heard the tragic news that Whitney Houston had died. "I was really sad to hear of Whitney Houston's death. It shook me up a lot. She is such a big part of my life. She was very inspirational, so it was really sad to hear that she had died. Growing up, I listened to Whitney, Mariah Carey, Aretha Franklin, Anita Baker and Nina Simone. Vocally, they all blew me away. It was lots of big powerhouse women."

While Emeli was deeply saddened by the loss of one of her all-time idols, she didn't have time to feel down for long. In just a couple of days, *Our Version Of Events* would finally be revealed to the world.

Upon the album's release on February 13, 2012, Emeli was in the middle of a promotional whirlwind, a maelstrom of live performances, interviews and in-store signings. At Glasgow's HMV, she performed a handful of songs to 400 fans, who had queued around the block, awaiting the chance to get their fresh-off-the-rack CD album signed by the singer. The acoustic set included album tracks such as 'Suitcase', 'Next To Me' and 'Hope', as well as the hit singles 'Daddy' and 'Heaven'. Emeli told the fans: "Thank you so much for your support. It's so nice to be back in Glasgow and to see so many familiar faces."

Upstairs in the HMV green room, she revealed she was all set for her BRITs night. "I picked the dress last week and my parents are coming down," she said. "They're really excited. It's a great way for me to mark the great year I've had and hopes for the year ahead, to have people that are important to me around me."

After the intimate in-store gig Emeli was whisked away by people carrier to make an appearance on Glasgow's Clyde 1 FM radio station on the outskirts of the city. The station, established in the seventies, sits in a complex in the town of Clydebank, home of eighties chart-toppers Wet Wet Wet. As the interview got under way, and with the album number one in the midweek charts, Emeli revealed that she had a typically humble celebration in mind: "If the album goes to number one on Sunday, there's going to be a little get together and we'll have a few drinks. I never, ever go out – people think I'm the most boring person in the world. They were all asking me, 'Are you going to go out to celebrate your BRIT?' But it's not me. Even at my birthday parties we all end up sitting about, writing songs. So some people have stopped coming because they know that's how it will end. I'm not into nightclubs, I get awkward in situations like that where there's too many people and you have to make small talk."

This was her big push and the moment of truth. She had been waiting for this moment for more than a decade.

Meanwhile, Emeli was quoted by the *Daily Star*'s Kim Dawson as saying that she wouldn't write any more songs for Simon Cowell's acts until he introduced himself to her. She had penned tunes for some of his biggest acts, including Cher Lloyd, Susan Boyle and Leona Lewis, and the music mogul reportedly wanted her to write for a new generation of *X Factor* contestants. Emeli said: "I'm going to try to do something for Simon. But I still have to meet him. We haven't actually been in the same room. I've only ever been approached through his people so it would be good to say hello. But if I get the time to write for his projects, I'd love to."

By now Emeli was also happy to open up about her songwriting with Alicia Keys. "We're writing for her next album and I go back out to the US at the end of the month to join her again. There's one song that we wrote together called 'Hope', which is on my album too. It's fantastic."

Keys, who became an international superstar following the release of her 2001 debut album, *Songs In A Minor*, kept three of the songs from the sessions with Emeli for her 2012 album, *Girl On Fire*. The collaboration which produced the tracks '101', 'Not Even The King' and 'Brand New Me' – may not be the last time the pair work together. "She's like my little sister," Keys said. "I think that's why we actually wrote so many amazing songs together. It's awesome to see a young artist grow and I feel proud I was able to be a part of her story because she's special. I love that we both play, sing and write. When you go into the studio with someone it either works or it doesn't. This time it really worked and there was a lot of conversation and planning together. I had some ideas I would play and she had some ideas she would play. It was awesome and so fluid."

Still, despite the flurry of success Emeli was experiencing with her music, she still hankered for the chance to return to uni. "For example, the other day I took out my old research project from uni simply because I wanted to revise for fun," she said. "I miss the library and all that type of stuff. It's turned out that my album comes out on the same day my finals would have been, February 13. I keep in touch with all my friends from uni on Facebook, so I've seen them all posting about their exams on there. It's so weird how it's all worked out – but I'd much rather be doing this than medicine finals." But Emeli didn't lose touch with academia completely, as an appearance with a difference that same week proved, when Emeli returned to London to take a music class for 70 students at the British Music Experience at London's O2.

Then, the moment was upon her. The following Sunday evening of February 19, 2013, just two days before the BRIT Awards, Emeli got confirmation that all the hard work had paid off. Along with millions of music fans, she tuned in to Radio 1 to hear the chart rundown, only to discover that *Our Version Of Events* had debuted at number one with a staggering 113,000 UK sales in its first week. As well as getting the news that she had gone all the way to the top of the charts, she was presented with a gold disc by her label for achieving over 100,000 sales. To top it off, *Our Version Of Events* was the second-fastest-selling album of the year. Having spent years trying to convince label bosses to give her a chance in her own right, she had finally made it, and on her own terms. "It's exciting because it's all about being credible again. The focus is on singer–songwriters now rather than huge shows. I mean, of course there's always a place for that too."

Still on a high from her BRITs Critics' Choice win and the nomination for British Breakthrough Act, she added: "It's a huge thing to see young people really appreciating melodies and songs again. I mean, there'll always be room for big productions and everything but it's good to see the other side. I watched Ed Sheeran recently and thousands of 16-year-olds were transfixed by him. It was only him and his guitar – it was an arena full of people."

And with her third solo single, 'Next To Me', sitting at number two in the charts, it was just the beginning of the journey for the star songwriter. "It was a song that came very quickly and I wanted it to be very simple," Emeli has since revealed. "When I'm singing it, I am singing it about different things depending on what I'm focused on at that moment. Sometimes I am singing it about my husband, because he's next to me and I feel his unconditional love. Sometimes I am singing it about God or love that's just there, and whether you call that God or whatever you want to call it, that's what I'm thinking about."

But having the album be received so well was the biggest thrill of all. "It was emotional to hold the CD. I was like 'Wow – this is 20 years of work'." She couldn't have imagined then that the album would go on to spend a record-breaking spell in the Top 10; at that moment, getting to the top was enough of a thrill. "The album coming out and going to number one was a very surreal moment. You work so hard, one, to convince people to work with you, to give you the chance and then you finally get it. Then there is a single, and every step takes so much of your energy, and so to finally put out a whole body of work and it goes to number one was amazing, especially after all the sacrifice you have to make to get there."

Looking ahead to the awards, she said: "But what's happening now makes it worth it. The BRITs will be something else."

Sadly the BRITs would, indeed, be something else for Emeli, but for all the wrong reasons.

In the early days, the Britannia Music Club sponsored the event, hence the name. Later, 'BRIT' became an acronym for British Record Industry Trust, a moniker that suggests a sedate affair, with elderly moguls puffing on fat cigars and murmuring their appreciation as each winner is wheeled out. But as anyone who has been to the BRITs or watched it on television knows, it is anything but sedate, even if the alcohol has occasionally been removed from the tables in recent years.

The Awards began in 1977 and became an annual event in 1982. They were televised in a live broadcast until the debacle that was 1989's ceremony, when Fleetwood Mac rocker Mick Fleetwood and former glamour model Samantha Fox presided over what has since been described as a "bun fight". Fox blamed a stuck autocue as the pair struggled to ad-lib their way through the event. Acts failed to turn up on time. Then there was the 16-inch height difference between the pair, which made the cameramen's job a thankless one as the shots hovered between Fleetwood's midriff, only slightly less voluptuous than the former Page Three model's attributes. And the whole shambles was broadcast live to the nation.

Thereafter, the BRITs were recorded until a decision was made to return to the live broadcast in 2007. In the intervening years, controversy and schoolboy-type shenanigans lurked behind every pillar. In 1996, Jarvis Cocker stormed the stage, lifted his shirt and pointed at his behind during Michael Jackson's 'Earth Song' performance. The Pulp frontman claimed to be protesting against Jackson's apparent presentation of himself as "a Christ-like figure".

Then there was the Britpop feud that saw Blur and Oasis trade insults from the stage that same year and, in 2000, Robbie Williams collected his awards for Best British Video and Best Single for 'She's The One' while simultaneously challenging Oasis frontman Liam Gallagher, who was out of the country at the time, to a fight. So when the 2012 Awards came along, the press were looking forward to what they hoped would be an eventful bash, despite the BRITs having become somewhat sanitised in more recent years.

And if they were looking for controversy, they got it in the form of Adele Adkins' middle finger. Choking back the tears after accepting the Best British Album award from George Michael,

Adele's big moment was soured when presenter James Corden cut short her acceptance speech to make way for closing act Blur. The crowd booed and Adele flipped the bird, making known her feelings towards the diss in front of a six million-strong TV audience.

For the media, it was a dream come true, and they jumped on what they saw as BRITs producers and organisers snubbing Adele in favour of the ageing Britpop act. The accusations of the British music industry being an 'old boys' club' came thick and fast. The *Daily Express* wrote "FINGER OF BLAME POINTED AT 'THE SUITS'" after Adele told reporters backstage: "I flipped the finger but it wasn't to my fans. I'm sorry if I offended anyone, but it was the suits that offended me."

Now another Adele was about to take her big moment on the BRITs stage the same night. Her proud mum and dad, having flown all the way from Aberdeen to be with their daughter on the greatest night of her career, were looking forward to seeing their daughter take to the stage and collect her Critics' Choice award. Instead, they were to be deeply disappointed and all because the organisers had to stick to a live schedule. While Ed Sheeran was crowned King of the BRITs – the ginger haired singer-songwriter celebrating wildly after scooping two gongs at the star-studded bash – Emeli sat at her table waiting for her big moment. But at no point was she invited to step onstage to collect her prestigious award, nor was it presented to her at her table.

The BRITs organisers' failure to pay sufficient tribute to the hottest new music talent in the UK might initially have gone unnoticed. But when the *Daily Record* asked why Emeli Sandé had been largely ignored, there was an awkward silence. While the BRITs team scrambled to get their story straight, Emily's PR, Gordon Duncan, got down to some straight talking.

Over the years Gordon has worked with artists ranging from the Spice Girls, Olly Murs, KT Tunstall and newcomer Jake Bugg, right through to the Killers, Bon Jovi and Snow Patrol. Even with such an impressive roster, he describes working with Emeli as a dream come true. The feeling is probably mutual, since he helped put Emeli on the map. "I knew from the start that she was special," he says of the star. "You don't hear a voice like that every day. From the start she has been an incredible act to work with. The fact that she is Scottish is a dream come true. She is different from the other acts I have worked with. Personally, I think she could become one of the most successful acts I have worked with from the start. That is especially satisfying, especially when she is Scottish and especially when she is really nice. As well as being incredibly talented she has a really good work ethic and understands that the music is only part of the story and she has to work hard to get that music across. In terms of the promo work she has had to do she has always been up for doing that. She listens to the people around her and she has said herself that she makes music because she wants people to hear it. She writes music because she wants to share it. You really do feel part of a team. She is at the centre of everything the promotion team does and she backs you up to help you do your job as effectively as possible. She understands the process of turning a raw talent into a global success, which is what we are on the way to doing. The journalists spotted from the start that she was really special as well. It has been satisfying from that point of view. The Scottish media understood from the start that this was a pretty rare talent and that she was going to go places."

Gordon also orchestrated a campaign for another Scots female singer-songwriter, Amy Macdonald. The campaign raised Macdonald's profile to the extent that her folk-tinged debut album, *This Is The Life*, sold four million copies, and she remains a million-seller to this day. If anyone would know how Emeli felt about being snubbed, he and her manager, Adrian Sykes, would.

The day after the BRIT Awards, the *Daily Record* ran the story that had everyone in the music industry talking, in a Scottish showbiz exclusive with a front-page splash headlined "EMELI TEARS AT BRITS SNUB". The report went on to state: "Scots singer Emeli Sandé broke down in tears when she was hit by a huge snub at the

BRIT Awards, we can reveal. The 24-year-old chart-topper was stunned after being denied the chance to accept her Critics' Choice award on the live TV show. A source said: 'Emeli received very poor treatment. She wanted to say thank you for the support she got. She is devastated she couldn't do that.' The snub at Wednesday's event was seen by millions of TV viewers."

What should have been a wonderful moment for Emeli was later described, diplomatically, as "an unfortunate TV moment" by her manager, Adrian Sykes.

And the reason for the apparent snub? The show was behind schedule and cuts were made, although that wouldn't explain the fact that Emeli wasn't scheduled to go onstage to collect her award in the first place, which surely would have been the appropriate way for her to celebrate her win. The ceremony organisers made things worse by preventing Emeli from speaking about her win on the live broadcast. Emeli had prepared a speech to thank those who had helped her. Instead, she was ignored. When the cameras cut to Jessie J, she was asked what advice she would give to Emeli, who was sitting just feet away with her parents, Diane and Joel, and her fiancé, Adam, at her side.

By asking "So what advice does Jessie J have for Emeli Sandé?" the *Daily Record* endorsed the fact that anyone with a brain could see Emeli's career was already beginning to dwarf that of the previous year's Critics' Choice winner. Of course, Jessie J wasn't to blame. She was merely trying to fit in with the wishes of the show organisers, and she wished only the best for Emeli.

Concerned about upsetting BRITs bosses, Emeli's entourage has remained tight-lipped about the incident to this day. But at the time, a source close to a devastated Emeli said: "I just think it was an almighty c**k up. I don't think it was deliberate. They dropped the ball on Emeli. She received very poor treatment. She has a number one album and they're asking Jessie J what advice she has got for her. Emeli's family were there and this was the moment when she should have been celebrating and having a nice time. Instead of talking to Jessie J, they should have been talking to Emeli at her table." The source added: "After all the hard work of the last year, she was really looking forward to having it officially acknowledged on the night in front of her family and friends. She wanted to say thanks for the honour and for the support she has received on the way. She is disappointed that she didn't get the opportunity to do that."

ITV's Director of Communications, Mike Large, eventually came forward to explain what had happened: "The decision was taken between the producers and ITV." And a source at the BRITs said: "Because there was more music than ever before, everything got pushed back. The BRITs love Emeli. They really support her and think she's fantastic."

In the days after Adele's Best Album acceptance speech was cut short, hundreds had called in to complain, leading ITV to issue a public apology to the 'Rolling In The Deep' singer. Writing in the *Daily Record*, Melanie Harvey said what should have been a celebration of two of music's best female talents had turned into a blokey love-in. "With awards for Adele and Emeli Sandé, the show had the chance to fly the flag for our females," her column stated. "Adele and Emeli have two of the best voices in the business, don't use their sexuality to sell records and are giving the guys a lesson in how to shift albums by the bucketload. So why were they allowed to be humiliated in front of a TV audience of millions? Adele was rudely interrupted during her – very short – acceptance speech to make way for 11 minutes of boys' boys Blur shouting their way through their Britpop hits from the nineties. Meanwhile, Scots singer Emeli was in tears at a table with her mum and dad, who had made the journey from Aberdeenshire for their daughter's night of glory. She had already received her Critics' Choice Award and wasn't invited on stage or allowed to thank her fans on live TV. Host James Corden didn't stop at her table. He did find time for a chat with Kylie, who wasn't nominated for anything but was looking glam for a gal in her forties. He also had a matey gab with Jessie J. She won nothing, so quite why she deserved airtime can only be explained by the producers of the ITV show."

It had been a major blow, but Emeli's upset was short-lived, thanks to the news that one of the world's biggest bands had made her an offer she couldn't refuse.

7. GOING FOR GOLD

The day after the BRIT Awards, and after the organisers issued an apology to Emeli for the 'snub' fiasco, the Scottish singer was able to put the heartache behind her with the news that Best British Group winners Coldplay wanted her on their US tour, from March. Not only was Emeli extremely flattered, but it was a chance for her to repeat her successes in the UK music industry over the pond in America.

As she boarded a London flight for New York on a cold February morning, Emeli used the news to put the BRITs upset behind her. "Nothing can take away from how happy I am about winning the Critics' Choice award," she said. "I was a bit disappointed with the way things went on Tuesday night at the event, especially as my family were there too. But my album's number one, my single's number two and I've got loads of stuff going on, so I really have nothing to complain about. I'm so grateful to be in this position and to have this kind of success already. It's all a dream come true." Her reaction was another display of the professionalism she'd shown throughout her short, but incredible career. But there was one hitherto undisclosed flaw, and that is that Emeli can be incredibly absent-minded: "I lose car keys and phones all the time. I have always lost things since I was a kid," she said. "I blame it on being creative. I lost a clarinet when I was a kid and I still lose things a lot. The [BRIT] award itself is such a great design. My manager has got my BRIT so I don't lose it. He is going to keep it safe for me. He's got my passport. I focus on the music. He takes care of everything else."

Naturally, Adrian Sykes had everything covered for Emeli's Stateside initiation, and Emeli was more than up to the challenge: "My parents are really excited about all my success and are trying to make sure I have enough time to take a break. I've had to explain that the next few weeks are going to be very busy. They're very proud."

By now, even some of Emeli's fans were having trouble keeping up with her accomplishments. As well as her previous solo hits 'Heaven' and 'Daddy', she had now amassed a raft of collaborative smashes with Professor Green, Wiley and Chipmunk. She'd also found time to work with urban star Labrinth on his debut album, *Electronic Earth*, released on April 2, 2012, lending her vocals to the track 'Beneath Your Beautiful' and had now completed her work with the original Sugababes line-up. But Emeli realised she had to put her own singing career first and not spread herself too thin.

"The collaborations will need to take a back seat at the moment, but I am really hopeful that when things calm down a wee bit I'll be able to spend a couple of weeks writing for other people," Emeli said. "But I have been writing for the Sugababes. That was one of the first things I agreed to do this year. That has been great fun and it is sounding incredible. I've been working with Labrinth. We are releasing a song together, which I think is beautiful."

Despite the increasing demands, to the extent that her management were fielding dozens of calls offering her work on a daily basis, Emeli still managed to make time to support causes close to her heart. In March, she returned to London to perform with Ed Sheeran at an event for the War Child charity, before joining Annie Lennox at the EQUALS Live show at London's Royal Festival Hall in the same month, an event promoting gender equality as part of International Women's Day.

"I love Annie Lennox," Emeli said of the chance to work with the powerhouse singer. "It was always an inspiration to know that someone had come from my city and made it worldwide. It's incredible that I will be performing at her event. I will get to meet her, which will be fantastic."

In a conversation with Lennox for *Time Out* magazine and in the spirit of the EQUALS Live event, Emeli revealed how important her dad had been in encouraging her to make the most of her talents. "My dad is from Zambia and he always made me and my sister feel very capable, and that you should be able to do anything regardless of where you come from or what sex you are," she said. "But I did study medicine, and there was a distinct view that women should be GPs and guys should become surgeons, because women are going to have a family to look after. In the music industry I've found there's rarely a woman who has her own music studio, or a room of her own. I'm a big fan of Virginia Woolf's essays about how important it is to have a real space of your own. I'd like to see more women behind the scenes in publishing and management."

And right then, Emeli had to draw on every resource of strength she could find to get through her bulging schedule. As well as the US support slot on the Coldplay tour, she was embarking on a "small, intimate" tour of the States in her own right that February. "I'm looking forward to taking my music there. This is where it starts."

She then planned to return to play more UK dates, including a homecoming gig at Aberdeen Music Hall followed by a show at Glasgow's Old Fruitmarket that took place on April 10. She was also lining up to play summer festival dates, including T in the Park, Lovebox and the Isle Of Wight festival. She was determined to cope with her meteoric rise from unknown medical student to in-demand singer and songwriter, all in a little over a year. "I'm pretty ambitious," she admitted. "I always reach as far as I can with what I am doing and want to get my music out there. The best piece of advice I have been given was from Tinie Tempah. He told me to sleep when I can because he is still exhausted from things he did last year. He warned me that things are going to get really hectic. It's just crazy. A year ago, I would never have imagined going to the BRITs and having a number one album."

On February 27 Emeli made her headline debut on a US stage, at the Box in New York City, with her US label in attendance: "This is my first gig in America," she said to the audience. "I'll always remember this no matter how it goes."

Keeping her fans back home informed, she tweeted afterwards: "My first concert in NYC! Another 1st. Had a great time performing last night!! My favourite way – small, acoustic and intimate! 1 more day in New York and the sun is shining!"

Capitol Records posted a snap of her gig, tweeting an enthusiastic: "Such an OUTSTANDING show! xo."

Emeli found some rare time to indulge in a bit of sightseeing the day after the gig, before meeting up with Alicia Keys, to work on more songs. Alicia counts the collaboration as the highlight of 2012. The 'Empire State Of Mind' star said: "'When we met and we really began to write together, it was instant magic and that doesn't happen all the time. There's about three songs on my album that we did together and they are, all three, unbelievably special.'"

Next, Emeli returned home to shoot a video with director Dawn Shadforth, known for her work on Kylie Minogue's 'Can't Get You Out Of My Head' and her promos for Oasis, Florence & the Machine, Goldfrapp and Garbage. The video would accompany fan favourite, the stunning piano ballad 'My Kind Of Love'. The emotional video sees Emeli singing while riding a carousel before visiting a terminally ill relative in hospital who she takes on a car journey to see the sights of their youth one last time. The moving footage suited the incredible emotion of the song and further cemented Emeli's status as Britain's hottest singer-songwriter.

She followed up the shoot by returning home to Glasgow to perform at the Scottish Variety Awards at the city's Crowne Plaza hotel, where she also picked up Breakthrough Artist of the Year. Her truly heroic work ethic rewarded again, next came the news that she would light up Glasgow as part of the city's 2012 Olympic

Torch Relay celebrations, to be held later that year. Scheduled to play Glasgow's George Square as part of 66 nights of celebrations leading up to the London Olympics, the free event would see her perform alongside Eliza Doolittle and indie rockers General Fiasco on June 8. Emeli said of the opportunity: "I found out a few days ago in New York that I'm going to be running with the Torch and that is really exciting and an honour to do. I think that's going to be a really special moment. Maybe tonight I'll just double-check I can do it properly. I'm trying not to think about falling over, the flame going out or my hair going on fire. It's great to celebrate the flame coming to Scotland."

Even closer to home for Emeli – a mere 25 miles from her hometown – was her return to Aberdeen for an emotional homecoming concert. The show had been postponed from its planned December 2011 date, due to clashing with her support slot on Coldplay's European tour, but the four-month wait was worth it.

Summer seemed to have come early that April, and unseasonably warm temperatures greeted Emeli as she entered Aberdeen's Music Hall for the show. Mum, Diane, dad, Joel, family and friends were among the full house who'd turned out to enjoy a singer at the top of her game. The crowd were hushed as she gave them 'My Kind Of Love' and 'Suitcase'. But the biggest applause followed her own version of 'Read All About It'. The closing highlights came with her first solo single, 'Heaven', and the uptempo 'Daddy'. Her Aberdeen debut now felt a world away. "Aberdeen was really emotional for me as Mum and Dad were there and the last time I played Aberdeen Music Hall was when I was a young kid with a recorder," Emeli said. "I went back and everyone was up for it."

Although Emeli was as focused as ever on putting on a good show that night, she admitted that it was an emotional event, and that she hadn't forgotten her Aberdeenshire roots and cherished her time in Glasgow, her next stop on the live gig roster and another homecoming of sorts. "I spent most of my time in places like Byres Road," she said of her downtime as a student at the University of

Glasgow. "I hope the record shop Fopp is still open because I did my new music shopping there. There were so many cool places like Murano Street in Maryhill. When I was doing my first year at med school, I remember being so stressed before my exams. I had a keyboard and was making up tunes and sending them to people. I wrote 'Diamond Rings', my first hit, in Hyndland as I was hoovering up. Someone sent me a beat and I was hoovering my room and trying to write while doing it."

Now, things were happening so fast, she admitted to having to pinch herself. "The first bit of the tour in Europe surprised me with the amount of people and how they knew my music. In the UK, people remember the words from the album and in the US, the crowd reaction is wonderful."

Back in Glasgow for an appearance at the Old Fruitmarket venue as part of her sold-out UK tour, she showed her appreciation for all the support she was receiving when she told the crowd: "Thank you for coming. Thank you for getting the album to number one. Thank you for the BRIT award. Thank you for everything." At the sell-out show, she also previewed 'Hope', one of the songs she had co-written with Alicia Keys, and a highlight from that night's performance.

Later she said of her return to the city: "It's amazing to be here and feels really nice. You can get caught up with how quickly life goes by in the music biz. But this brings back memories of my whole struggle and puts things in perspective about how far I've come."

It wasn't just the Scots who appreciated Emeli's talent. In the Welsh capital, her show was met with equal enthusiasm. The Cardiff university student's union gig was yet another intimate and important UK date in which she was able to show her fans that she could cut it on the live circuit.

And when the tour reached London's Shepherd's Bush Empire, Emeli told the audience: "Thanks for making my dreams come true." Here, she opened with 'Daddy' and described 'Clown' as "a song which says you'll have the last laugh eventually". Having faced rejection on numerous occasions before finally landing her record deal, her smile said it all.

As summer progressed, it was time for the Olympic Torch to make its way to Scotland, and Emeli would be there to serenade its arrival. But before the historic shows, and despite her busy schedule, she found time to attend a charity show 40 miles west of Edinburgh, in Glasgow.

Each year in May, Our Heroes, an awards ceremony organised by the *Daily Record*, celebrates the heroic achievements of Scottish people from all walks of life. Despite her enormously busy schedule, Emeli still had time to attend the event, which that year was held at Glasgow's Thistle Hotel, along with her mum, dad and publicist, Gordon Duncan. She explained her decision to perform at the dinner: "[The nominees] are the real heroes because they don't get awards, although on this occasion they are. They're not the people we read about in the papers. They're not doing it for any kind of glory. They're selfless people and help others out. You can only admire that. Personally, I think it is incredible. All the doctors and nurses I used to see, and the families of patients, were great. You never hear about those people who come and show support and real love in those tough situations. My heroes include my mum who has been really supportive of everything I am doing and always made sure I had as many opportunities as possible. From my experience, that's true of all mums. She would be my hero. My music teacher at primary school, Mrs Simpson, was also a big hero of mine. She was my teacher from Primary 2 and made music really exciting."

When it came to listing her creative heroes, Emeli had clear favourites. "Of the famous people who have inspired me I'd have to say Nina Simone. She is a big hero because she was so out there with her music. She was a really big inspiration. I have a tattoo of Frida Kahlo on my forearm because I was blown away by the Mexican artist's portraits. She was very brave in what she created and was unapologetic for who she was. She inspired me to make music in the same way. She gave up a career in medicine as well and chose art, which inspired my choice to follow my real passion. It is not easy to do something you feel is true and you are passionate about, so for Nina and Frida to wave the flag for women in the creative industries back then was a big deal."

Emeli went on to sing two of her hits to the delighted nominees and guests, which she described as "an inspirational night", before Capital DJs Clark and Jennie Cook surprised her with her own award, for Scotland's Entertaining Hero. Emeli said of the honour: "I really wasn't expecting to feel this support from people in Scotland. It's really lovely as this is where I feel most comfortable." Six months later, Emeli would perform another charity concert on behalf of the Prince's Trust, at London's Royal Albert Hall.

However, before that, in June, crowds gathered to witness the Olympic Torch as it made its journey through Scotland. And Emeli would play an integral part in the string of celebrations. At Glasgow's George Square, she described the experience of taking part as a once-in-a lifetime opportunity. "I studied here for about five years so it's so nice to come back ... and I can feel the excitement." She beamed proudly as she held the Torch aloft in Glencoe, less than 24 hours after singing at the Glasgow bash and before another Olympics celebration concert in Inverness. By now, she had played a string of short gigs to welcome the Olympic Torch to the cities of Scotland, but if she was fatigued she didn't show it. Only when asked about her gruelling schedule did she let slip that she was running on empty. "It's been exhausting," she said. "But I've got a great team and I haven't worn myself out yet. I'm booked up until Christmas now."

The centrepiece of the torch relay's journey through Scotland came on June 13, at Edinburgh Castle. The castle is a fitting venue for such a unique celebration. The fortress towers above Scotland's capital, dominating the city's skyline. In the 12th century, David I took up residence, and the castle played a major part in historic conflicts, from the Wars of Scottish Independence in the 14th century to the Jacobite uprising of 1745. These days it serves as an iconic tourist attraction; the Edinburgh Military Tattoo takes place there as part of the annual Edinburgh Festival in August and it also occasionally serves as a venue for rock and pop concerts. Rod Stewart, Runrig, Bob Dylan, Elton John, Il Divo, Paul Simon, Tom Jones and James Taylor have all played there, usually thanks to the work of Edinburgh-based promoters Regular Music. Now it was Emeli's turn to take to the Castle Esplanade stage, and her performance would beam live around the world.

During the concert she declared: "It's an honour to be here tonight." This final date in the series saw her performing with a saltire painted on her cheek, as she performed four hits including 'Heaven', 'My Kind Of Love', 'Next To Me' and 'Wonder'.

Days later she became torch-bearer number 47 as the torch made its way to the RockNess music festival. "I don't think within my lifetime we're going to be able to do this again, have the Olympics in my country, so it's definitely something I'll look back on and it will always be a fond memory," she said of the historic occasion. But little did she know those fond memories from the Scottish Torch Relay were merely a warm-up to an already balmy Olympic summer.

8. A SPORTING CHANCE

By the end of June, Emeli was continuing to impress critics on both sides of the Atlantic with her incredible work rate. The summer US dates with Coldplay were just around the corner, and she had already secured a slot on the American late night television talk show *Late Show With David Letterman*. "Letterman will be amazing," she said, "and I've got some VH1 shows and the Coldplay tour in stadiums during the summer Stateside, which is really cool."

Her own Stateside shows were beginning to draw plaudits from the critics. CBS News ran a review under the banner "UK's Emeli Sandé charts her own success with debut", while Bloomberg ran the headline "Adele, Aretha get upstaged as Emeli Sandé plans invasion".

"We started very slow in America. It was small acoustic shows," Emeli said. "We played places like Los Angeles, New York and Chicago and everywhere there has been a great reaction. It has been really lovely. They listen to the lyrics and the melody over there and the reaction has been fantastic. It's a good feeling and it feels like it's bubbling. It's a good time to come to America."

The rave reviews coincided with Emeli collecting yet another award, at the Nordoff Robbins 37th Annual Silver Clef Awards, held at London's Hilton Hotel on Park Lane. Joining Emeli, who was awarded the Silver Clef Music Innovation award, at the star-studded ceremony were Kylie Minogue, who was awarded an honoree 25th Anniversary O2 Silver Clef Award, and music impresario and composer Andrew Lloyd Webber, who was honoured with the Sony Mobile Lifetime Achievement Award. Jessie J picked up the gong for Royal Albert Hall Best British Act, while other winners included rising star Conor Maynard (TAG Best Newcomer Award) and Michael Bublé (Raymond Weil International Award).

By now, Emeli had sold 532,000 copies of *Our Version Of Events*, making it the UK's second-biggest-selling album of the year, outsold only by Adele's *21*.

Despite the balmy temperatures that greeted Emeli earlier in the year on her return to Scotland for the Olympic Torch Relay concerts, summer 2012 ended up being one of the wettest Scottish summers on record, which didn't bode well for the upcoming T in the Park festival. It had rained day after day for weeks in the run-up to Scotland's biggest music weekender, held at Balado near Kinross. Today, almost 90,000 people make an annual pilgrimage to the Scottish music event, which was first held in 1994 at Strathclyde Park, Lanarkshire, on a much smaller scale. But the 19th T in the Park, held on the second weekend of July, lived up to its potential as a total mud bath. In the artists' village and press tent, members of the press could be heard making jokes about trench foot and, after laughing at one photographer's shot of a naked male reveller on his back in the mud, similar afflictions to other parts of the anatomy were also predicted.

Scotland's largest festival had recently won the Best International Festival accolade at the coveted Pollstar Awards in Los Angeles. But in 2012, the glamour of LA seemed a long way away as 90,000 hardy revellers endured some of the worst conditions in the festival's history, including flooding and bucket loads of rain. Thankfully, the T in the Park audience is renowned for generating bucket loads of atmosphere, and the crowd made sure that every one of the 100-plus acts playing the sodden stages received a rousing welcome.

Among those who succeeded in lifting the crowd's spirits despite the damp were the recently reformed rockers the Stone Roses, Noel

Gallagher's High Flying Birds and Scots dance star Calvin Harris. Emeli, low down on the bill, drew a very respectable crowd, in spite of the lakes of mud that would be in direct contrast to her return in 2013, which coincided with a record-breaking heatwave.

Having made her debut performance at the festival and now back in the artists' village, she hinted at her motivation to continue apace with her gruelling schedule. "I'm being asked to play a lot of festivals in the UK, and in Scandinavia and Europe," she said. "It's going to be a fun summer. It's important to get the balance right. I'm still a new artist so I need to do as many shows as I get offered. But at the same time it has to be the right thing. I'm not going to turn up if a crowd isn't going to be my kind of audience. T is my sort of audience."

Performing to tens of thousands may have been a step up for Emeli, but if the crowd at T in the Park seemed colossal, it would be dwarfed by Emeli's next big gig. Just a fortnight later, Emeli Sandé would perform to the world.

That summer, Great Britain was in for a treat. For the first time since 1948, Britain was to host the Olympic Games, and by July 2012 anticipation was at fever pitch. And the 10,500 athletes from all over the world, competing in 26 sports, did not disappoint. The entire country was swept up by Team GB mania and was well rewarded, with Great Britain hitting the highs of the medals league table, coming third only to the USA and the People's Republic of China. The event was crowned by Super Saturday, which saw golds for Mo Farah, Jessica Ennis, Greg Rutherford, and from the river and the velodrome, leading to Great Britain's best single day at any Olympics in over a century.

But the breathtaking displays weren't confined to the sporting arenas.

On the evening of Friday, July 27, Brits all over the UK arrived at street parties, ready to celebrate the opening night of the London Olympics 2012. Some chose to have gatherings at home, while others simply plonked themselves in front of their television sets to catch what would be a unique evening's entertainment ahead of the global sporting event itself.

For weeks the press and public had speculated over the content of the Opening Ceremony; with film director Danny Boyle in charge and amid rumours that the participants had been made to sign confidentiality agreements, the press clamoured for sneak previews. But in the days preceding the event and once the dress rehearsals had begun, news of a theme started to emerge. It was to be the glue that made Britain great, from the NHS to Winston Churchill's indomitable spirit that led the defeat of the Nazis in the Second World War.

When the lights went up on the 80,000 seat Olympic Stadium, all of the speculation fell to one side as it quickly became clear that Boyle had created a spectacular show with a cast of thousands for an audience of billions. 'Isles Of Wonder' was a celebration of what makes Britain great, and the best of British were keen to make an appearance, even if the take-home pay was a mere £1 (enabling them to enter into a contract with the organisers). Holding the Olympic Torch aloft, footballer David Beckham arrived in a speedboat which whizzed along the Thames, while Sir Paul McCartney readied himself for the biggest audience he'd ever faced in his illustrious 50-plus year career. Even Her Majesty the Queen got in on the act, appearing as a 'Bond girl' opposite the current 007, Daniel Craig, who could be seen in a pre-recorded segment walking the corridors of Buckingham Palace, corgis at his feet, before coming face to face with the reigning monarch. Good on Her Majesty for allowing a stunt double to parachute into the stadium from a helicopter high above the ecstatic crowd.

For the most part, thousands of volunteers were expertly choreographed to provide a dazzling spectacle, surrounded by magnificent props and stage sets. And in among the extravaganza was one person, quietly awaiting her turn on the giant stage.

Emeli Sandé was an unknown singer just a year before. But now she was about to captivate a global audience in one of the standout moments of the ceremony. And she would do it all with just her voice, such was the subject matter she was dealing with. During a montage dedicated to the 52 victims of the London 7/7 terrorist bombing of 2005, Emeli sang the hymn 'Abide With Me'. Few could have carried off such an emotional tribute, let alone a singer who who was still very much in the ascendancy. But Boyle and the ceremony musical directors, the British electronic music group Underworld, trusted she could carry it off. And she did more than that, providing one of the most moving pieces of a show full of tear-jerking moments. "I've always loved that song. It's one man's message to God as he dies," Emeli said, of Scottish-Anglican writer Henry Francis Lyte, who composed the hymn just three weeks before his death from tuberculosis in 1847. "When we met, Danny and Underworld took me through the whole ceremony and I hoped that was my part. When they said it was, I had such trouble not telling anyone."

As she stood in the middle of the Olympic Stadium, not so much solemn as serene, the nation paused and watched and, no doubt, the vast majority realised after a few short moments that they were witnessing a real artist; that this was a special performer who could stop the clocks and fill the audience with an incredible sense of occasion. There's surely no argument that Emeli delivered an emotional punch through the simplicity of her performance that night, in stark contrast to what had gone before. For some the performance epitomised longing and loss, while for others it was comfort, and yet others it was a combination of all of these emotions. Whatever it was that the Scottish siren exuded as she sang 'Abide With Me', one thing was clear: Emeli had arrived on the world stage. From now on, there surely would be no need to explain who this bouffant blonde from Aberdeen was. She had stolen the show at the opening of perhaps the biggest sporting occasion in the world while forgoing all the razzmatazz and bluster often employed by superstars with less talent. She had ignored the potential for trickery, forgone the vocal gymnastics so often served up by newcomers like an overblown CV, or rather Danny Boyle and Underworld had dispensed with the need for it. This was a raw performance: both poignant and powerful.

But while she appeared calm and assured under the gaze of billions, Emeli was anything but at the rehearsals for what turned out to be the professional highlight of her career so far. "That was a huge moment," she said. "And the most nerve-racking of my life, not just the year. Partly because at the dress rehearsal, in front of 16,000 people, my mic wasn't working. "I was trying not to think about how many people were in the stadium and also how many people were watching at home and the fact that the Queen was out there. It was quite mind-blowing. I was very nervous and I don't think I'll feel that nervous again. I definitely felt the responsibility of the song. The lyric of 'Abide With Me' is so personal to so many people, so I think that was making me more nervous than anything. However, I felt very calm when I stepped out. You can't really see people, you can only see lights. Everybody went very quiet. It was like being underwater."

Though thrilled to see her daughter perform to the biggest audience of her career, mum, Diane, worried that she was doing too much, too fast. "Sometimes I get a bit worried about how tired she must be with all the travelling. The pace of things is a bit frightening," she said. "For Emeli, stepping out at the Olympics in front of all those people must have been scary, but she seemed to cope with it."

Someone else who waited with bated breath for Emeli's performance that night was Laura McCrum, who had witnessed the young Emeli impress the cleaners during her soundcheck at Aberdeen's Lemon Tree venue some years before. "Seeing her sing at the Olympics I just sat there and the tears were streaming down my face. It was complete pride through and through," she said. "As I watched her performance I had flashes of her as the 17-year-old girl, growing up, studying and committing to music. It became a standout memory for me."

Amazingly, this was only the beginning of Emeli's association with the London 2012 Olympic ceremonies. Sixteen days later she was back, along with a cast of 15,000, at the Closing Ceremony. This time, the show was masterminded by artistic director Kim Gavin – the man behind Take That's record-breaking Circus tour – and he'd lined up a stellar cast of the biggest names in the history of British music, including rock A-listers the Who and the Kinks' Ray Davies, ex-Wham! star George Michael, and pop groups Madness and the Spice Girls, the latter having reformed for the occasion. This time, Emeli performed 'Read All About It (Pt III)' on a moving stage, a truck wrapped in newspaper print, which circled the arena.

Some months later, Emeli looked back on her experience that summer. "Danny Boyle asked if I would come and meet him to speak about the Olympics and next thing I knew I was singing at the Opening Ceremony and the Closing Ceremony. So that year was quite mental."

Trevor Nelson, who commentated on both ceremonies for the BBC, considers Emeli's performances to be a crucial point in her career. "I was really keen to see how she would handle it. All of us didn't know it was going to be as huge as it was. But still, for an artist, it is bigger than getting an *X Factor* final on a Saturday night. At least twice the size of that. As an artist, these are the moments in your career you can't dream of. You don't know if they are ever going to exist. It's like doing a Superbowl half-time performance. She did both the opening and closing ceremonies so effortlessly and I saw her in rehearsals and on the night when it all happened and we all realised, 'This is it. What's going to happen?' She handled it so well."

The only drawback to that monumental night would be a decision by US television channel NBC to replace the tribute to the 7/7 victims with a bland Michael Phelps interview conducted by Ryan Seacrest. The decision led to a flood of criticism on Twitter.

"It is a shame the American viewers didn't see her sing 'Abide With Me' at the opening," Nelson said. "But everybody else was blown away with how she just takes it in her stride. She is a class act and I think that makes her a star. She's a star purely on substance. I really mean that. I don't want to throw other names out there. But look at Kylie Minogue, for example, who is a star but it is a completely different thing and from a different country. Emeli is not a Kylie, she is not a Britney, and Lady Gaga is a different thing. Well Gaga is quite talented. She writes her songs and does her stuff, but Emeli is different. Emeli is stripped down and old fashioned. She says, 'I'll write you a song and you'll get that song just through delivery' and that is a star. It's so obvious to everybody."

An example of her stripped down and old-fashioned style has never been more evident than on the outstanding version of 'Abide With Me' she recorded in one take at Capitol Studios' studio B, the video for which can still be found online.

If Emeli wasn't already a household name, she would be after those Olympics appearances, certainly in the UK. In fact, many of the artists who performed at the Olympic ceremonies saw huge spikes in record sales. Sales of the Spice Girls' *Greatest Hits* album rocketed 626 per cent after their Closing Ceremony stint. Emeli enjoyed a 476 per cent boost for her own album, which sent it back to the number one spot. Sales of the album had now overtaken Adele's *21* by 3,200 copies, making *Our Version Of Events* the biggest-selling album of 2012. Emeli was also riding high in the Singles Chart with 'Read All About It (Pt III)'.

Even if her status as pop music's "best kept secret" was well and truly out, there was still the chance to see this superstar in the making in an intimate venue when Emeli performed at the 3,000 capacity Camden Roundhouse as part of that summer's iTunes festival.

But what *was* still a best-kept secret was the wedding Emeli was busy organising. It was dad, Joel, who leaked the news on Twitter. "Just about to embark on a 4hrs flight to hand my older daughter's hand in marriage. Feels surreal but great. Here's hoping everything goes to plan. It's been a great year."

The Scottish singer, having turned 25 four months earlier, planned to wed her "toy boy", Adam Gouraguine, that September in his homeland of Montenegro. But thanks to dad, on the morning of the wedding Emeli's manager, Adrian Sykes, found himself fielding a flurry of calls from journalists he promised to get back to after his four-hour flight from London to a wedding location he had hoped to keep under wraps. Later that evening he confirmed that Emeli was in Montenegro and she would indeed be marrying Adam the following day in a ceremony for "family and friends" that they were "trying to keep as private as possible". But the wedding was anything but subdued. It was a fairy-tale affair, the bride's dad and her sister, Lucy, arrived by boat at the exclusive Porto Montenegro Marina before Joel walked his daughter up the aisle.

"I was very pleased about the wedding," Joel said afterwards. "It was nice to get [Emeli] married in Montenegro. I felt very proud. I did give her away. The groom had gone ahead with the party and Emeli, Lucy and I came on a yacht. I delivered her to the altar and handed her over to Adam. I did a speech on the night. Traditionally, they shoot guns in the air but on this occasion it didn't happen at all. There were no guns."

Diane added: "I think Joel is being a bit shy. The wedding was in one of the most beautiful locations. It was by the sea. It was very chilled and very relaxed. Montenegro is gorgeous. A lot of her uni friends and people she had known for years from Glasgow were there along with music people she knows and works with. It was fantastic."

Joel couldn't have been happier with how the day panned out. "It was fantastic to finally get them to make honest people of each other," he said, tongue firmly in cheek. "I mean, they had been together quite some time. Seven or eight years is quite a long time and I was getting a little bit worried that they might end up living together as partners."

Following the exclusive ceremony, Emeli took once again took the opportunity to sing, this time at a free concert for locals in the town of Kotor. During a previous trip to Montenegro with Adam, when she was still relatively unknown, Emeli had managed to fit in a concert in the country's second-largest city, Nikšić. But that wasn't the first time Emeli had performed in Montenegro, having made an appearance in the south-eastern European country while still an unknown singer. "It was one of my first gigs outside the UK. I was very nervous about performing in front of such an unfamiliar crowd," Emeli said. "I even had my speeches translated between songs. I was anxious to how they would react to my style. It turned out to be an amazing show. The crowd were really moved and showed me so much love."

In fact, the show generated so much attention that she was interviewed in one of the country's national newspapers and the national news. "It was an unforgettable experience and showed me that music can be used to break down cultural and racial barriers," she enthused. "I think my music brings real honesty and truth. I have no intentions to be cool or hip for a certain time period. I feel these qualities are rare in the music industry at present, which seems to be so contrived. My music has no target audience. It's open to everyone and I think that's because we can all relate to something truthful."

This time, Emeli was interviewed for Montenegrin TV, where she revealed: "I want to be part of his life and his family, so I want to add his surname. I would also love to have a Montenegrin passport. I want to be part of his tradition. I grew up in a family of two different cultural backgrounds, so I embraced both. One day when we have kids, I'd like them to be the part of these two different cultures."

Now going by the name Adele Emeli Sandé Gouraguine, the singer singled out her wedding day as the highlight of an incredible year. "Getting the album out was a big thing that I had wanted to do for so long, so that was a big highlight when it got to number one. Doing the Olympics and getting married were big highlights. Getting married is huge. For me, it was the perfect day. Everything was exactly how I wanted it to be. It was such a beautiful day and one of the best I have ever had.

"I've been lucky. I've married my best friend. Since I was 17, we've been together. But we've had ups and downs," Emeli revealed. The young couple would be following suit by not rushing into the next stage of their relationship: "I don't think I'll be having children for a long time," Emeli said of her decision to focus on her burgeoning career.

However disappointed Northsound 1's Gary Muircroft was that Emeli couldn't make it into the station to collect her Contribution to Music In The North East award, he believes she had a pretty good excuse, the honour having been scheduled in the wake of her nuptials. "She couldn't make it," he said. "We didn't know why but it turned out she was getting married and was going to be on her honeymoon. Her mum attended and accepted the award on her behalf and Emeli sent a video. There was only one winner from the North East that year. She had performed at the Olympics!"

Soon after, the long-awaited collaboration with Leona Lewis was finally unveiled: Leona's new single, 'Trouble', which Emeli had penned for the *X Factor* winner's third album, *Glassheart*. The two singers had also collaborated with Naughty Boy and Fraser T Smith, the producer behind albums by Adele and Florence & the Machine. Leona said: "I became friends with Emeli after Tinie Tempah got in touch with me. Tinie sent me her song 'Trouble'. It was in a raw demo form. I got together with Emeli and said I really liked her idea."

During a rare moment of simple pleasure, Emeli and Adam returned to London after their honeymoon to attend the *Skyfall* premiere in London. Emeli admitted she hadn't ruled out following in Adele's footsteps and singing a Bond theme in the future. "It's a legendary thing to do, so I think I'd absolutely love to do it," she said. "I'd be well up for the challenge. It would be really cool."

But Emeli was fast becoming a legend in her own right, beating Adele and Noel Gallagher to win Best Solo Artist at the 2012 Q Awards on October 22. "Getting the Q Award was great after all the work that I have put in this year having paid off. I was there last year and I lost out on Best Newcomer. It was great to be in a room full of icons at the Q Awards, which is a magazine that has supported me from the very beginning."

Days later, with five MOBO nominations – a haul matched only by British rap and soul artist Plan B – Emeli walked away with the trophies for Best Female Act, Best R&B/Soul and Best Album.

Among the star guests at the MOBO Awards was soul legend Dionne Warwick – who was honoured with the MOBO Lifetime Achievement award that year – who said: "I really, really love Emeli's voice. She's wonderful. She's a star."

"It's been a crazy year for me," Emeli said of the whirlwind that was 2012. "But I think it's so important to stay true to who you are and remember where you came from and the people who helped get you where you are. MOBO supported me from the early days of my career so to pick up three awards is so special. I really didn't expect to win three, and getting the album of the year was a big thing for me, so I feel like all the hard work pays off when you get acknowledgement like that."

Meanwhile, she was about to compete against some tough competition in the charts – herself – as Naughty Boy's 'Wonder' found itself pitted against Labrinth's 'Beneath Your Beautiful', both of which featured Emeli on vocals. Both tracks also appeared on a deluxe version of *Our Version Of Events*, which would be released just in time for Christmas. "It's been a really incredible week," Emeli said at the time. "The Labrinth single wasn't supposed to be released for another few weeks and it is hopefully going to number one." In fact, after Emeli and Labrinth performed the track on *The X Factor*, the song jumped to the top of the iTunes Top 10 overnight.

Meanwhile, Emeli continued to support a favourite charity: her tour included a huge date at Glasgow's Clyde Auditorium on November 6, 2012, from which she donated a chunk of the ticket sales to music therapy charity Nordoff Robbins. "I wanted to give back to charities that have allowed me to come to their buildings and see what they are doing. I'm an ambassador for Nordoff Robbins and seen what they do, so it made sense for the proceeds to go to their great work. Because of my background in medicine, and my love of music and the music therapy Nordoff Robbins do, it's a special charity to me."

As the busiest year of her life was drawing to a close, Emeli was looking forward to spending time back in Alford with her family at

Christmas. "I don't think I'm going to be with [Adam]. I'm going up to Aberdeenshire and he's going home to Montenegro, so I won't see him. But we'll be in Dubai for New Year because I'm doing a show there, so that will be nice.

"I try to go home every year for Christmas. Everything shuts down in the music industry at that time of year and I just get to go home – it's great to get back every year. But she revealed she wouldn't be putting her feet up entirely: "I guess when I'm back at home I'll try to write as much as I can. It's difficult to find the time," she admitted. "I've been writing songs for a few people. It takes so long though, from the writing to recording and the songs being released. It's a long process."

In an interview with *The Sun*'s Niamh Anderson before her Clyde Auditorium Glasgow show, Emeli spoke of her hopes for her trip to the States in the New Year: "New ambitions are to take things international. You have to approach the States in a different way to the UK. It's so big and so vast that you have to build up from the grass roots again. I'm signed to a label over there and I'm really chuffed that I have a team in place who understand me as an artist and my music. Taking my music to the rest of Europe and America, and to work on the second album, is the next step. With this career it never stops. You can never draw a line and say you have completed everything you wanted to. I have to prove myself again with a second album and establish myself as an artist."

And Emeli was also enjoying establishing herself as one half of a married couple. "It's nice to have the stability and go home and know that's your man. Whatever happens he's got my back and I've got his. We live in London now but we have so many memories in Glasgow. He proposed at the last MOBOs here, so it's a city with lots of memories for us. Being married is great. When everything's going crazy in my career, it's nice to feel secure at home. I feel very grounded."

Emeli did seem very relaxed backstage at Clyde Auditorium, perhaps because the show she was about to perform would kick off her last tour of the year at home in the UK. She talked of how she missed Glasgow, being a student and the communal feel of the city's West End. She reminisced about her concerts at the Old Fruitmarket. She also revealed details of another songwriting commission – this time for pop/R&B singer Rihanna. 'Half Of Me' would appear on the Barbadian superstar's 2012 album *Unapologetic*. Rihanna reportedly cried when she heard the song.

Before Christmas came round and Emeli got her break at home, she had one last chance to impress the public when Simon Cowell invited her to perform as a special guest on the 2012 *X Factor* live final. It was also a chance to prove one of her previous detractors had made the wrong choice about her.

In the lead-up to 24-year-old singer James Arthur being crowned winner of the ITV talent show, Rihanna, One Direction, and then Emeli took to the stage. The song she chose to perform on ITV in front of a viewing audience of 11 million was 'Clown', and it earned her a standing ovation from the studio audience and all four judges – including Gary Barlow. The Take That star made no mention of having previously met Emeli, let alone turning down the chance to sign her to his label, Future Records.

Naughty Boy sat in the audience, aware of the irony that the lead judge on Europe's biggest talent show had failed to recognise the hottest female star in the UK. "Emeli's performance [at the Future audition] was identical to how she performed the song at the *X Factor* final. Barlow shouldn't have said what he did [at the audition] because it could have knocked Emeli's confidence and she could have walked away from music."

Just days after Emeli's *X Factor* performance, Barlow announced he was closing Future Records to spend more time with his family.

By now, Emeli's album had spent 43 weeks in the Top 10, so it was no surprise when T in the Park boss Geoff Ellis confirmed the Scottish siren for the festival's 20th birthday celebrations taking place in the summer of 2013. As she was being announced for T, Emeli was also added to the bill of another concert, the SL20 Concert at London's O2 Arena on April 18, 2013, which would mark an entirely different 20th anniversary: that of the murder of 18-year-old Stephen Lawrence. For those unaware of the case, in 1993, Stephen, a black teenager from south-east London, was murdered at a bus stop by white youths chanting racist slogans. Years later, the failure of the police to properly investigate the killing led a public inquiry to conclude that the force handling the case was institutionally racist. By agreeing to take part in the concert, Emeli's social conscience was once again in evidence.

But for now, she had the Christmas holidays to think of. Emeli spent Christmas, as she had done much of the year, at the top of the charts. *Our Version Of Events* had now reached almost one million sales when she appeared on *Jools' Annual Hootenanny* on BBC 2 to herald the bells at New Year. In another example of the magic of television, Emeli was seen celebrating with Petula Clark, Bobby Womack, Paloma Faith, the Hives, Jake Bugg, Kevin Rowland from Dexys Midnight Runners and the Dubliners ... even though she was thousands of miles away in Dubai.

If Emeli felt 2012 couldn't get any better, there was more cause for celebration as 2013 began. Less than a week into January, the Official Charts Company announced that she had made the record books. With *Our Version Of Events*, Emeli had claimed the record for the most number of consecutive weeks (47) in the UK's Official Albums Chart Top 10 for a solo debut album. At that point, only the Beatles' *Please Please Me* had spent longer in the Top 10, at 62 consecutive weeks. By now *Our Version Of Events* had also spent a total of seven weeks at number one.

Official Charts Company managing director Martin Talbot said: "In her first year since winning the BRITs Critics' Choice award last January, Emeli has truly established herself as a new British star. Her debut emerged as the biggest album of Christmas 2012 and the year as a whole. This new chart record further cements her in that position."

As if things weren't happening fast enough it was only days later that Emeli discovered she had been nominated for three more BRITs to add to her Critics' Choice award from the previous year. The nominations included Best British Album, British Female Solo Artist and Best British Single nods for 'Next To Me' and her collaboration with Labrinth on the song 'Beneath Your Beautiful'. The news was an example of just how far Emeli had come in such a short space of time. As she prepared to release her new CD and DVD package *Live At The Royal Albert Hall*, she said of her nominations: "It's a really good feeling. It feels great, a bit scary, because you never know, you might not win anything."

If Emeli was struggling to keep her feet on the ground, it wasn't because she was getting carried away with her incredible successes; it was because she was jetting off for her US tour. "It's exciting," she said. "We'll go from state to state and hopefully build a following. There's still a lot of pressure, but I work best under that. I'm excited about trying to win them over."

So with 'Clown' now in the singles chart and her album still at number one in the UK, it was time for Emeli to have another go at the US market or, at the very least, get more of the stateside critics on board.

As the London-based 25-year-old was travelling across the Atlantic, fans back home jammed phone lines and braved the cold outside Aberdeen's Music Hall two hours ahead of the box office opening for Emeli's homecoming gig. Joyce Summers, press manager with Aberdeen Performing Arts, said tickets for that April show sold at breathtaking speed. "We always knew it was going to be a hugely popular gig," she said. "Emeli has an enormous following in a city. People regard her as one of their own. We drafted in extra staff to cope with the calls."

For Emeli the appearance would be just as important: "I'm very excited, as always, to be coming back and playing in Aberdeen – but this time will be extra special as we finish the UK tour."

A second Aberdeen gig, which would be held three hours before the original show at the same venue, was announced to meet demand. It too sold out within minutes.

With all that was going on back home and the US tour to think of, Emeli chose that moment to announce yet another expansion of her incredible career. She and Naughty Boy planned to set up their own record label to help those artists being ignored by the majors. Having faced difficulty getting signed herself, Emeli explained what the label meant to her: "It's about how I felt when I was trying to get signed, when I was going for all these meetings and people were looking at me like, what do we do with you? I built a reputation as a songwriter before my own hits. People were coming to me for songs. I wanted to keep songs like 'Clown' and 'Mountains' to sing myself. But the record labels saw me as a songwriter. It was hard to get people to believe in me."

Among the artists Emeli and Naughty Boy had chosen to work with was Ella Henderson, a 2012 X *Factor* contestant. "I've always been a massive, massive fan of Emeli," Ella told *Heat* magazine. "I'm in awe of her for songwriting reasons. I'm meeting with her soon. We've spoken but not met face to face. It feels so weird that I'm coming into a world with an artist I respect."

So, Emeli's long-term plan was to help showcase other emerging talents and gain control of her destiny through her own label. Her destiny in the US was still unclear, but a free concert at LA's Key Club for the revamped MySpace social media site must have won her brownie points with her American fans. The event at the Sunset Boulevard nightspot was streamed online for 24 hours after the event, with movie star Joseph Gordon-Levitt and fellow *Inception* actor Lukas Haas both in the crowd.

In Emeli's absence and less than 10 days before the BRITS, she won Best Music Act at the *Elle* Style Awards 2013, but couldn't attend the ceremony to collect her trophy as the American appearances came thick and first. She appeared on ABC's late-night talk show *Jimmy Kimmel Live!*, where she sang 'Heaven' in a black dress and glossy red biker's jacket at a time when she was still experimenting with her style. She also performed on the *Today* show, yet she felt she was still scratching at the surface. "You really can't go over there for a month or two, you know, you really have to invest a huge chunk of your life to make it happen. I think if you put out great music and you're patient and willing to put the work in, it'll work out. For me it's like two years ago in the UK. You go to the shows and it's just that real raw excitement at the beginning, when people have just found you as an artist. I love that and it's a brand new challenge for me and I'm enjoying it."

A week before the BRIT Awards, Emeli continued to create that "raw excitement" when she appeared at Clive Davis' annual pre-Grammy party at the Beverly Hilton Hotel in Los Angeles. And the appearance provided her with another opportunity to perform for one of her idols. Among the A-listers at the party, including Usher, Patti Smith, Jennifer Hudson, Gladys Knight, Johnny Depp, Sting and wife, Trudie Styler, and Joan Collins, was Joni Mitchell. The veteran singer-songwriter loved Emeli's performance, telling FOX411 entertainment news columnist Roger Friedman: "She's a real artist."

Emeli also guested on talk show *Ellen*, before Sir Elton John's AIDS Foundation (EJAF) announced it had selected the Scottish singer to perform at the 21st Academy Awards Viewing Party on Sunday, February 24, 2013, at West Hollywood Park – four days after she was required to attend the BRITs. Moreover, Elton – who has championed new talent throughout his incredible career – spoke of his love of Emeli's music and his belief that she would soon be just as popular in the US as she is back home in the UK. "Emeli Sandé's album, *Our Version Of Events*, is a true work of art and a favourite of mine," said Sir Elton. "When she is on stage, you can feel her passion for music and the heart that goes into her lyrics." In a statement to the world's press, he said: "I can't wait to introduce Emeli to my guests and experience her live performance together. I predict that by next year she will be a multi-Grammy award winner."

...neli performs as part of HMV'S Next Big Thing at London's Borderline on February 9, 2012.
AMIR HUSSEIN/REDFERNS

Emeli performs during the London 2012 Olympic Games Closing Ceremony at the Olympic Stadium in London on August 12, 2012.

...meli poses with her Best Solo award in the press room at the Q Awards 2012, held at the Grosvenor House Hotel on October 22, in London. DAVE M. BENETT/WIREIMAGE

Newly wed Emeli and her husband Adam Gouraguine attend the *Harper's Bazaar* Women of the Year Awards 2012, at London's Claridge's Hotel on October 31.
DAVE M. BENETT/GETTY IMAGES

...meli and long-term collaborator Naughty Boy at the launch of the MOBO awards 2012. WENN

Emeli performs at the second Annual Budweiser Made in America Music Festival during Labor Day weekend at Benjamin Franklin Parkway in Philadelphia, PA. SPLASH NEWS/SPLASH NEWS/CORBIS

Emeli poses in the awards room at the 2012 MOBO awards at Echo Arena on November 3, 2012 in Liverpool, when she won Best UK Female, Best R&B/Soul Act and Best Album awards. SHIRLAINE FORREST/GETTY IMAGES

The Literary and Historical Society at UCD presented Emeli with the James Joyce Award. WENN

T In The Park Festival, Balado Kinross-shire, Scotland, on July 12, 2013. DANIEL GILFEATHER/REX FEATURES

Sandé arrives for the 2013 Echo Music Awards in Berlin, Germany, March 21, 2013. JENS KALAENE/DPA/CORBIS

Sandé performs at the V Festival, Chelmsford, Essex, on August 18, 2013. KEVIN ESTRADA/RETNA/CORBIS

Emeli is awarded the best British Album award during the BRIT Awards, at the O2 Arena in London, February 20, 2013.
DYLAN MARTINEZ/REUTERS/CORBIS

Emeli on the red carpet at The Clive Davis and The Recording Academy's 2013 Pre-GRAMMY Gala at The Beverly Hilton Hotel in Beverly Hills, California. SALANGSANG/LEP/SPLASH/*SPLASH NEWS/CORBIS

Emeli is awarded the honorary degree of Doctor of the University from the University of Glasgow on June 12, 2013. Emeli received the degree for her 'outstanding contribution to the music industry'. GLASGOW UNIVERSITY/SPLASH NEWS/CORBIS

Emeli sings happy birthday to Tinie Tempah at his album launch party at DSTRKT on November 7, 2013, in London. PHOTO BY DAVE J HOGAN/GETTY IMAGES FOR BEATS BY DRE

Emeli in concert at The Fillmore, Miami, America, October 11, 2013. JOHNNY LOUIS/REX FEATURES

"I'm absolutely delighted to have the chance to work with Sir Elton again and to help support the amazing work he continues to do with his Foundation," Emeli's statement read. "I was lucky enough to perform at his Winter Ball recently and I'm sure this will be as memorable a night. I look forward to helping the Foundation raise funds and awareness for those touched by HIV/AIDS."

Mum, Diane, and dad, Joel, admit they have to pinch themselves as Emeli's career continues to reach new heights. "It seems like a daydream, to be honest," Diane said.

And still the collaborations poured in, with former *X Factor* contestant and 20-year-old rapper Misha B revealing she had been working with Emeli. "I've co-written with Emeli on my new album. She's super cool. I've met Emeli quite a few different times. She's just very inspirational, to see her journey just grow and grow and grow, and it's all through the love of music and her message, with her music touching people."

A year on from her Critics' Choice award win, Emeli was no longer the underdog when 2013's BRITs came around again. Betting firm Paddy Power had given odds of 1-6 for Emeli to collect Best Album and 1-10 to be named British Female Solo Artist. Adele's 'Skyfall' Bond theme was odds-on favourite to win in Emeli's other category, but no matter what the bookies said, nobody in Emeli's camp was taking anything for granted, particularly after the minor setback of the previous year when she was overlooked when it came to collecting her Critics' Choice award.

But this time everything went just as Emeli, her parents, husband, Adam, and her management team must have hoped as she was crowned the undisputed queen of the BRITs. Her phenomenal climb to the top continued apace as she won two of her categories, claiming the gong for British Female Solo Act and beating off stiff competition from Mumford & Sons, Alt-J, Paloma Faith and Plan B to take the Best British Album award for *Our Version Of Events*.

As Bryan Ferry handed Emeli her second award of the night for Best Album, she said: "I think I am a very unlikely pop star. You know, this is an album I wrote because I didn't have the confidence to say those things in person. That so many people found strength in these words makes me feel incredible. *Our Version Of Events* is our truth and at the end of the day that is all we really have. I was hoping to connect with people. To know that many people have gone out and listened to the words and told their friends is really encouraging. It makes me want to make something else, and it feels wonderful. What I remember most about making the record was being an underdog. That was the most exciting thing. It was that hunger, not so much for success, but for people to listen. We had to try so hard to go against people who said it was no good. I remember having that defiance and I loved it. It was great."

That night, Emeli also provided the climax to the BRITs night by closing the show to a standing ovation with performances of her hits 'Clown' and 'Next To Me' in an O2 Arena filled with music business executives from both sides of the Atlantic and fans who had purchased gold tickets to see the show. It had been exactly 12 months since BRIT organisers had failed to properly acknowledge her Critics' Choice win. Emeli's double win and performance was made all the sweeter because her family were there to watch her triumph. And finally Emeli could let her hair down: "When I'd heard I won [Best Album] it was an incredible feeling. It'd been such a year of hard work. That award was one I really wanted, and I was up against some incredible albums. I had my family there, so I felt very, very happy and celebrated quite a lot that night."

Making the "rabbit run" of waiting press and media in her Dolce & Gabbana dress, she admitted: "I was nervous all night. I knew I couldn't get drunk until I performed. It's a dream year. When you're eight years old you think of these type of years. For all of these things to happen to me, I feel very grateful. I'm glad the risk of leaving med school paid off."

It had been over 10 years since she had performed in front of Richard Blackwood at the Rapology showcase, and he was impressed by just how much she had achieved in that time. "If you think about her look with the blonde hair, she is now a package. Even if you are not sure who she is, if you say the girl with the blonde hair people know. This goes back to the years she spent learning her craft, sometimes voluntary and sometimes involuntary, in the sense that I'm sure when she was younger she wanted to be successful back then. Now she has made herself distinctive and the BRITs had to pay attention to her. I remember going onto iTunes and they were promoting her like crazy so I bought the album. Next thing she won the BRIT awards. Whoever is behind her has marketed her in such a right way that she is undeniable. I'm glad for her. Last year, I saw her on the MVAs. Once she gets international stardom that's it, and I think she'll make it. She really will."

As congratulations poured in, another, more surprising message arrived, as Emeli later revealed: "Everyone's emailing you. Because my husband's from Montenegro, we got a message from the President of Montenegro, which does quite stand out. It felt incredible."

9. AMERICAN DREAM

On top of messages from world dignitaries, Sir Elton John had also given Emeli his vote of confidence he invited her to perform at his 21st post–Academy Awards party. The glamorous annual party, which attracts the biggest names in showbiz, was held at West Hollywood Park in Los Angeles. For Emeli it was the chance to perform at the gala in front of some very influential people, including legendary producer Quincy Jones. But the performance had a deeper meaning; the party is the largest fundraising event in Hollywood on Oscars night, regularly raising over £20 million for the Elton John AIDS Foundation (EJAF), a cause that Emeli supports. "I sang for the Foundation in London a few months ago, so I'm a big supporter and it's just such a big cause for me," she said, prior to her performance at the Oscars party. "My father is from Zambia, and over there AIDS is such a horrible and massive problem."

As it turned out, the room was also filled with major artists supporting EJAF, including Miley Cyrus, Britney Spears, Aerosmith's Steven Tyler, the Foo Fighters' Dave Grohl and film director Baz Luhrmann. Emeli, who had previously performed at Elton's Winter Ball, was delighted to get the chance to work with the legendary singer–songwriter again.

"I had a great time. Introducing my music over here is always fun," Emeli told *Rolling Stone* magazine after her performance of 'Next To Me' to a room full of celebrities. Impressed by the fact that she shared a table with Sir Elton himself and U2's lead singer, Bono, she said: "I wouldn't have believed it last year, let alone when I was a kid. You have to take a moment to let it all sink in and not move so fast that you don't realise what an insane night that was."

But stardom waits for no one, and while the media crowned Emeli the "musical highlight" of the night, both Sir Elton and Bono promised to help her break America. The plan was simple: she had to spend as much time in the States in 2013 as possible and win over the Americans, one by one if she had to. Irishman Bono was generous with advice for the young singer from Scotland.

"We were sitting next to each other discussing the Oscars, and I was asking him questions about when U2 first came over to the States," Emeli said. "It was really kind of crazy, now that I think about it. Bono talked about the first album – he was saying you tour, you keep plugging it. And Elton was the same. He was talking about how he was opening up for different people and all the little showcases they did here at the beginning. It was really encouraging and just cool to have their support."

By now Emeli had already decided to spend as much of the year in the States as possible in an effort to push *Our Version Of Events* to American audiences. The trip also created more opportunities for collaborations. "I worked with [hip hop artist] Kendrick Lamar, which was really cool. I met Jennifer Hudson at the Clive Davis party and we're hopefully going to do some writing together. To write for someone with such an incredible voice is always very rewarding."

But, having taken the same baby steps with Chipmunk, Wiley and Tinie Tempah on her way towards solo stardom in her own right, did it concern Emeli that she'd have to feature all over again in the States? "That's the way I started in the UK," she said. "I was featuring a lot, just trying to get my name anywhere I could. I guess I am starting from scratch again. You've got to get your basics from the ground up. I love collaborating. I love hip hop. I do, because it's courageous. Those are the people making real music I think."

Even without the feature spots, there were indications that Emeli was already making inroads into America's heartland. "There have been a lot of people coming up saying congratulations [for her three BRIT awards], and it's not always people from the industry," she said. "I love coming back, and each time it feels like more momentum is building."

By the time March made way for April, another hint that Emeli's American star was on the ascendancy came in the same week she was nominated for two Ivor Novello awards back home.

The highly popular musical comedy *Glee*, a Fox television series about a group of ambitious McKinley High students who compete with each other via the medium of song, has enjoyed a string of top honours, including a Golden Globe, and is now regarded as a cultural phenomenon. It is also a worldwide smash hit. So when Broadway legend and Tony award-winning actress Idina Menzel performed a duet of one of Emeli's songs with *Glee* co-star Lea Michele Safarti, it had the potential to be a big deal. In the episode 'Sweet Dreams', Rachel (played by Safarti) is seen preparing for a Broadway audition when her mum, Shelby (Menzel), turns up to offer support. She suggests she sing Emeli's song, 'Next To Me', and the climax sees the pair give the song an upbeat spin to a piano accompaniment.

When the programme aired during the second week in April, celebrity gossip columnist Perez Hilton was there to give a blow-by-blow Twitter commentary. Hilton, famed for breaking the showbiz mould and delivering his gossip to the masses in the digital age (he has over six million Twitter fans and millions more readers of his blog), is well known for his cheeky irreverence, which sometimes borders on the offensive. On this occasion, however, he abandoned his usual tongue lashings, revealing instead that he was blown away by the 'Sweet Dreams' episode. His blog followed up with the headline: "Lea Michele & Idina Menzel Belt Emeli Sandé's Next To Me Causing Pure Glee!" He went on: "Seriouzly, Gleeks. We knew the track was goosebump-worthy. But after watching these two perform, we've gone WAY over the edge. And there's no going back... Rachel Berry got her mom back last night, even if just for an episode, and it was FABOUSH!"

As Perez waxed lyrical about Emeli's *Glee* debut, a preview of the soundtrack to director Baz Luhrmann's *The Great Gatsby* revealed that the Scottish singer had turned her hand to movie soundtracks, too. Luhrmann worked with hip hop's biggest star Jay Z, who served as executive producer for both the album and the film, for two years, re-imagining the vibrancy and immediacy of the Jazz Age for modern audiences via a blend of hip hop and traditional jazz.

For some time, it had been reported that Jay Z's equally superstar wife, Beyoncé, was a fan of Emeli's, but it was Jay Z who finally got the Scottish singer-songwriter into the studio, for the *Gatsby* soundtrack. And there was no better producer to lead her through a version of Beyoncé's mega-hit 'Crazy In Love' (which Jay Z had also produced and featured in back in 2003). Backed by the Bryan Ferry Orchestra, a jazz ensemble founded and led by singer Bryan Ferry, Emeli's version of the track once again showed her versatility as a recording artist.

Other contributors to the impressive soundtrack included Fergie, Lana Del Rey, will.i.am and Jay Z himself, on the track '100$ Bill'. Naturally, Beyoncé got in on her husband's act too, duetting with Outkast's Andre 3000 on a cover of Amy Winehouse's 'Back To Black'. This was the sort of company Emeli, who had struggled to hold on to her dreams of stardom at times, was keeping these days.

While the soundtrack was being previewed on the internet in a series of 30 second snippets, another new Emeli song, 'Call Me What You Like', had been leaked on the internet without her knowledge. Today, the leaking of songs is commonplace and often the public can be excused for suspecting a track has found its way online to help create a buzz ahead of an artist's upcoming release, but on this occasion there was no real benefit to having what was clearly a work in progress being brought into the public domain, and Emeli showed her frustration when she tweeted to her fans: "I have no idea how this song got leaked. Hmm."

Emeli took a break from her work in the US when she returned to Scotland for the two sell-out shows in Aberdeen on April 19, providing her closest friends and family with the chance to catch up on tales of her globetrotting. As she arrived in the city, she revealed she was glad to be back: "It's always special when I get the chance to go back to Aberdeen, and I can't think of a better place to finish the UK tour than in my hometown. I'm looking forward to performing for family, friends and fans and I know that with both shows selling out quickly, it promises to be a special day and gives me the opportunity to say 'thank you' to all those people who supported me at the beginning of my journey."

Her comment was another example of Emeli's determination to remain rooted and not get carried away with her incredible success. But some things were changing.

It was around this time, in March 2013, that one critic noted that Emeli was "dabbling in electronica" in her song 'Here It Comes', which graced the soundtrack of the film *Trance*, which was directed by *Slumdog Millionaire* director Danny Boyle. And, on the verge of becoming an international superstar as well as a homegrown one, her image was starting to change, albeit subtly. In the weeks preceding the Aberdeen Music Hall shows, style columnists commented on Emeli's slimmed down, glam look, complete with revamped hair and make-up, which had coincided with her latest assault on the States and the performance at Sir Elton's Oscars party.

Days later, on April 22, Emeli travelled to London to attend a memorial service for Stephen Lawrence at St Martin-in-the-Fields Church on the 20th anniversary of his death. It had taken almost 19 years – until January 2012 – to bring two of the gang, Gary Dobson and David Norris, to justice for the racially motivated killing of the black A-level student, who had been stabbed to death at a bus stop in Eltham, south-east London. Now Emeli was standing shoulder to shoulder with those demanding a fairer society, including Stephen's brother Stuart, his mother, Doreen, the Commissioner of the Metropolitan Police and Prime Minister David Cameron. With her mohawk swept flat across her forehead, Emeli arrived in sombre black for the memorial and for once something that had come naturally throughout her time in the spotlight failed her: she struggled to force a smile for the cameras. But within hours of her attendance at the memorial, Emeli had used the poignant service as inspiration for another song. She arrived home and changed out of her daywear, threw on a comfy jumper and sat down near her piano to strum her acoustic guitar. The words to 'Drop It Low Make It Rain', a ballad about pain and loss, came quickly. "After the memorial service, I was inspired to write this," she tweeted, describing the song as a "work in progress". She cheered herself with the thought that she would be returning to the USA within 48 hours. "The next step is New York, America. I know it's going to be hard work. I know it's going to be a big challenge, but I'm very excited about the journey ahead. I'm starting from scratch out there, from day one, square one."

That wasn't exactly true, unless having Jay Z invite you to sing one of his wife's songs for the soundtrack to the eagerly anticipated new movie from Baz Luhrmann was "starting from scratch". Admittedly, though, the States has often been an uphill challenge for British acts and on Wednesday, April 24, Emeli arrived at Heathrow airport, excited about the trip. "We're all packed and ready to go to America," she said as she approached the check-in desk, passport in hand ahead of her MTV *Upfront* show at the Beacon Theater on Broadway.

Having cleared customs at JFK, manager Adrian Sykes was in ebullient mood during the drive into Manhattan for rehearsals. "We're back, baby," he declared. "This is Emeli Sandé taking over New York."

Emeli had barely stepped foot in the Beacon Theater for rehearsals for the following day's show when she got yet more good news; 'Next To Me' had just gone gold in America. But even as she concentrated on making her mark in the States, Emeli had laid the groundwork for another chart hit back in the UK.

Again, it was all down to her incredible work rate, which didn't look like petering out. Three months earlier, when she had attended the BRITs Nominations Launch Party at London's Savoy Hotel, she'd stayed just long enough to fulfil her promo duties and hear that she had picked up four nominations before jumping in a cab for a five-mile trip across town to Hackney for another recording session. This time it was to lay down the vocals to two songs with British four-piece drum'n'bass act Rudimental, at their Major Tom Studios. The year before, Rudimental had enjoyed their first number one hit with 'Feel The Love', featuring John Newman, and they were now in the midst of recording their debut album. Rudimental's Leon Locksmith said: "...that shows what sort of woman she is, that she would drop all her plans to come to the studio and drop two massive tracks on the album. We were on a tight schedule and she nailed it in six hours. I think she has just got a love and passion for music and she has shared the same love we have for soul music. With that in our minds, it was inevitable that we should come together."

And Emeli showed once again that she is one of the most talented singers to come out of Britain in a long time. "[She] was like a breath of fresh air," he says. "It was funny because the rest of the boys were recording with her in the studio and I walked in on a session. I actually thought it was a CD playing, but she was standing in the booth singing her heart out. She was pretty close to perfection. On the flip side she is such a lovely person to work with. She is very genuine and a really good advertisement for Scottish music and Scottish vocalists."

Eventually, Emeli would feature on the hypnotic album tracks 'More Than Anything' and 'Free', which closes the album. The collaboration might never have come about had Emeli not been stubborn enough to be allowed entry to a Rudimental gig in London the year before. She had turned up to see the band, but a mix up meant she wasn't on the guest list and the gig was full. But she waited patiently until one person left and she was allowed in. Locksmith said: "She came to one of our gigs to listen to us or see what we were about. We didn't know she was coming. She struggled to get through the front door, but eventually I think our manager sorted it out. Then she came up to us and said she really liked the show and said she really wanted to work with us."

But if she hadn't got into the gig, Emeli and Rudimental would both have missed out on the chance to work together later that year. That third week in April 2013, as Emeli enjoyed new levels of success in the US and while Rudimental were back at the top of the UK singles chart with 'Waiting All Night' (featuring Ella Eyre), the collaboration was about to pay dividends. Rudimental's debut album, *Home*, become a massive hit when it was released the following Monday, but it would be overshadowed by a unique achievement. The day before the Rudimental release, on Sunday, April 28, Emeli's own debut broke a new record, one held by the Beatles for almost 50 years. *Our Version Of Events* had spent more consecutive weeks in the UK Top 10 than any other album in chart history. The achievement, confirmed by the Official Charts Company, revealed the Fab Four had spent 62 weeks inside the Top 10 with *Please Please Me* in 1963 and 1964. Emeli's album had now sold 1.82 million copies and had been in the Top 10 for a staggering 63 weeks. Having been the biggest-selling UK album of 2012, 429,000 sales racked up since the New Year also meant it was 2013's biggest seller.

"What a phenomenal day," Emeli admitted on hearing the news. "I'm completely lost for words and this is something I could only have dreamed of. The Beatles are the greatest band of all time and their legacy lives on and continues to inspire all of us that make music. I'm so happy that so many people have connected with the stories and the songs on the record. This really is our version of events now."

Once again, there was no time for Emeli to bask in the glory of her latest achievement as within the week she joined the A-listers at *The Great Gatsby* premiere in New York's Avery Fisher Hall at the Lincoln Center for the Performing Arts. Lining up on the red carpet along with stars of the film and soundtrack, her fairy-tale rise to fame ramped up another notch and must have made her UK triumphs seem almost parochial in comparison. Lead actor Leonardo DiCaprio, suave as ever in a dark blue suit, joined an equally suited and booted Tobey Maguire, rap mogul Jay Z and the film's director Baz Luhrmann, while actress Carey Mulligan looked stunning in a strapless red Lanvin mini-dress. Emeli also stunned in a black lace body-con dress, her trademark blonde locks shaped into a twenties-style side parting to suit the occasion. She walked the red carpet in strappy heels and posed for the battalion of photographers and videographers, who were there to capture the stars of the re-imagining of F. Scott Fitzgerald's great American novel. Returning to her hotel room and still buzzing from the experience later that day, she admitted: "I feel so inspired. This whole week has been incredible."

When the Ivor Novello Awards took place that May, Emeli was so in demand that she failed to attend to collect her awards for Best Song Musically and Lyrically for 'Next To Me' and Most Performed Work. She left it to fellow Scot Gavin Rossdale, charismatic frontman of the British band Bush, to collect the awards on her behalf. Fresh from celebrating his own Ivor for International Achievement, Rossdale heaped further praise upon the rising star. Comparing Emeli's trajectory to that of Adele, he said: "If anyone is primed for that kind of success it would be her because she's pretty amazing."

Her absence at the Ivor Novello ceremony was an indication that Emeli was beginning to crack the States. That week in May, she would perform at the *American Idol* finale results show. Emeli joined 19-year-old finalist Amber Holcomb onstage at the Nokia Theatre in Los Angeles to sing a duet of Emeli's now global hit 'Next To Me', in front of the judges, live audience and millions of viewers.

And just days later, Emeli could tick another American venue off her gig list: the White House. Having been invited to perform in front of US President Barack Obama and First Lady, Michelle, at the most famous address in the United States, Emeli took time out to pose under a large bronze bust of Abraham Lincoln and oil paintings of past presidents, including George Washington, before joining the other stars there to honour legendary singer-songwriter Carole King. King was there to receive the Gershwin Prize for Popular Song, awarded by the Library of Congress, and she was the first woman to do so, joining previous recipients including Stevie Wonder, Sir Paul McCartney and Paul Simon. Emeli joined pop singer Gloria Estefan and country superstar Trisha Yearwood for a rendition of King's classic 'Will You Love Me Tomorrow'. She also sang a solo rendition of another King classic, '(You Make Me Feel Like) A Natural Woman', before which she told the recipient of the award: "Carole, you're such a hero of mine and it's such an honour to be here this evening and play this wonderful song, so thank you so much."

Afterwards, Emeli admitted the invitation to perform rivalled playing at the Opening Ceremony of the Olympics. "Carole has really inspired me since I was really young, so that was up there," she said.

By now, Emeli was well on the way to cracking the notoriously tricky American market and she'd already made the *Billboard* Top 30 with her single 'Next To Me'. The fruits of her labour? Not a fast car, like the Ferrari fellow million-selling Scottish singer Amy Macdonald had bought: "I splashed out on a Yamaha Baby Grand piano, on which I keep the awards."

Sadly, no matter how well Emeli was doing on the international stage, it wasn't enough to impress the judges of the Scottish Album of the Year Awards. Although she was longlisted, Emeli didn't make the final shortlist of the 10 best albums recorded by Scots in the previous 12 months, despite *Our Version Of Events* having dominated the charts, gained a couple of BRITs and broken a record held by the Beatles for 50 years. Instead, the million-selling record had been edged out by 10 other albums by Scots acts such as the Twilight Sad, Admiral Fallow, Stanley Odd, Meursault and eventual winner, RM Hubbert, who won for *Thirteen Lost & Found*. With Calvin Harris also losing out to the shortlisted acts, Emeli would have to take consolation in the fact that the omission had been a controversial one and certain industry figures had her back. Scottish band manager Malcolm Blair, who looks after Alesha Dixon, Little Eye and Mark Angels, said: "I'm not taking anything away from the bands on the shortlist, but in terms of album sales, I don't see any of those bands selling much outside of Scotland at a more international and global level. In Scotland, too many bands think being successful is being underground and cool and trendy. It's totally parochial."

Scottish radio presenter and DJ Jim Gellatly said: "It's disappointing. Both Calvin and Emeli's albums are wonderful as pieces of art."

Having been ignored for an award in her homeland, Emeli would have to comfort herself with the news that her US ambitions were about to receive a boost: the singer had won Best International Act at the BET Awards in Los Angeles. Held in the Nokia Theatre and hosted by comedian Chris Tucker, with performances by Justin Timberlake, Stevie Wonder Chris Brown and R. Kelly, the event was another superstar-studded affair, with actors Jamie Foxx and Forest Whitaker among those presenting.

The summer was hotting up, and July kicked off with another short US tour, starting in Orlando, Florida, and consisting of just five shows. In Atlanta, Georgia, Emeli spent the evening of July 4th – American Independence Day – performing at the city's Tabernacle, during which she debuted new song 'Who Needs The World'. Having performed in Atlanta seven months earlier, Emeli admitted she enjoyed a warm reception from the Georgia fans. "We loved Atlanta," she said. "Before that I had been to the north, but it was my first time for Atlanta and the crowd really stood out. People had told me that it was a warm city and they were right. People were just shouting out and it felt like church."

By now, however, she had realised that making it in America would prove just as tricky as making it in the UK, if not more so. "It's a big challenge, but I always expected it because it's such a massive place," she admitted. "It's a whole other culture for me. You have to approach things from grass roots up, not just 'Here's an album' and expect what happened in the UK to happen there. It's challenging, but I'm really enjoying it. There's progress every time I come over."

But, despite the difficulties, Emeli told Access Atlanta that she was enjoying every minute and reaching the heights of the previous summer: "[The Olympic ceremonies] were the biggest things I've done and such special evenings for me. But there have been so many performances, I don't know if I can say that was the highlight, but it was just so massive."

At the start of July, Emeli then travelled to New Orleans to perform in the Ford Superlounge of the Mercedes-Benz Superdrome as part of the Essence music festival, an event originally established as a one-off in 1995 to celebrate the 25th anniversary of the magazine of the same name, which is aimed primarily at African-American women. Relaxing backstage, she was buzzing from having met another soul star she had grown up listening to. "On the way here I literally bumped into Brandy," she said. "We are trying to get into the studio to write together. I love her, so that's a big moment for me." She also made time for a special photo shoot that would make the magazine's August edition, in which she wore a DKNY dress and Otar Iosseliani necklace and revealed the secret of those blonde locks: René Furterer Okara Light Activating Leave-in Fluid.

Admitting the success of 'Next To Me' in the US had been a pleasant surprise, Emeli said: "Coming to the States was a brand new adventure to me so I didn't know how the radio worked or if people were going to like it. So I'm just taken aback that people really connected to the lyric and the positivity of it. I love singing that song because you see people thinking of someone that's loyal in their life."

Emeli also announced her second single release and follow-up to 'Next To Me' in the US would be 'My Kind Of Love': "You want to go to the next level and you want to keep going, but there is a reason for bringing out each song," Emeli explained. "You've got to make sure that you love it and that other people love it. In Scotland, it was kind of like I was flying the flag for myself. In London, there is a bigger scene. In America, it's on another level. To have a festival and people out to see soul music is amazing. I'd never seen that before, so you can't really compare the scenes."

Meanwhile, one of the most renowned Latin artists, Alejandro Sanz, joined Emeli on a remixed version of 'Next To Me'. With 9.5 million followers on Twitter and 22 million album sales, Sanz would help Emeli to connect with a new audience, particularly as he sang in Spanish on the track. For now, though, it was off to Texas for a streamed concert at the Austin City Limits stage.

She also made time to return to Scotland, in July 2013, for the country's biggest festival, T in the Park – this time as a major act on the main stage. Before her arrival, she took stock of her career so far. "It's great to have success and to be able to make more music. But I think if I changed and you become distracted, then your music ultimately changes and it becomes something that really isn't that important any more, because you're really just speaking about yourself," she said. "I want to make sure that the focus is to create something that can speak for others. The whole of last year was just such a crazy ride for me. I feel like it's really surpassed my expectations and it's gone a lot quicker than I ever would have imagined. I think people will be surprised how energetic I can get on stage. But I like to mix that energy with real intimate moments. I like to keep everything live and everything created on stage. I hope they feel inspired."

A year earlier, Emeli had attended the summer festival when it was a mud bath. Scotland's weather has always been unpredictable, but few could have guessed the weekender would enjoy 29°C temperatures and blanket sunshine. Having performed without the need for rainwear, Emeli once again caught up with friends and family in the festival's artists' village, and posed for photographs before heading straight to London for an almost identical gig at the Wireless festival, this time as the penultimate main stage act ahead of Jay Z's headline slot.

Next on the schedule was another trip to the States, this time to appear on *America's Got Talent* to duet with Labrinth on their UK chart-topper 'Beneath Your Beautiful'. Labrinth, real name Timothy McKenzie, had become the first non-talent show artist to sign to Simon Cowell's Syco label in 2010 and the duet on Cowell's US equivalent of *Britain's Got Talent* gave his single a huge spike in sales, sending it from number 38 to 5 in the US iTunes Chart in a matter of hours.

Having already enjoyed a massive success as the guest on Labrinth's single 'Beneath Your Beautiful' in the UK, Emeli said: "I was speaking to Lab when we did *America's Got Talent*. There's a moment when we had to spin around holding onto each other. That was a special, intimate moment that I'm never going to forget. Everything over there is so big. It's hard not to feel like you're just this little drop in this massive ocean. Being over there with Labrinth... that support was fantastic. The way people are responding to the music is really encouraging."

Perhaps it was a sign of just how far she had come when America's *Fuse* magazine declared that Emeli had "broke out Stateside" with her platinum-selling single 'Next To Me' and was now "helping a fellow Brit launch his career on this side of the Atlantic".

Once again, gossip guru Perez Hilton was on hand to praise the singer and her collaborator. "America, meet Labrinth. Labrinth, America," he posted. "You're going to want to know who this guy is, since he is MUSICAL PERFECTION!!! The AH-Mazing Emeli Sandé helped introduce her fellow UK-er on *America's Got Talent* Wednesday night, performing their duet 'Beneath Your Beautiful'. The song went to #1 in England and is now shooting up the charts here in the States! Less than 24 hours after their performance on *AGT*, the single has skyrocketed to the top 10 on iTunes! So...ready to have an eargasm?" Adding the cherry on top, NBC gave Emeli a spot on the *Late Night With Jimmy Fallon* talk show, recorded at the Rockefeller Center in New York.

August was already shaping up to be a particularly busy time for Emeli. Having attended the Moët & Chandon 270th anniversary party in New York City, Emeli flew back to the UK in order to do what she loved best, perform live, this time at the V Festival alongside headliners Kings of Leon and Calvin Harris.

She was also ready for a return to the UK Singles Chart.

'Lifted' rocketed straight into the Top 10 the following week, and this time it was Naughty Boy who got to take centre stage, with Emeli revisiting the role of featured artist. Both turned up at Capital FM to discuss the third single from Naughty Boy's debut album, *Hotel Cabana*, Emeli admitting that Naughty Boy, or Sha as she called him, was her favourite of all the people she had collaborated with. "He worked on the whole *Our Version Of Events* with me," she told breakfast show presenters Dave Berry and Lisa Snowden. "He is my favourite person to work with, so we know how we work together. We know the sound that comes out. It's really natural. I love it."

Naughty Boy had earlier had similar high praises to bestow on his musical partner. "Emeli is heavily featured [on *Hotel Cabana*] and that would never have happened without the work we did with Emeli's album and her success. I never feel like I'm in the background. I feel like what we have set out to achieve is more. The music and the message was key for us."

Having signed a publishing deal with ATV Music in 2012 and a recording contract with Virgin EMI, Naughty Boy's second single from the album – 'La La La', featuring Sam Smith – had topped the charts in May 2013. The song became one of the biggest-selling records of the year, ahead of the release of the album itself. Naughty Boy also revealed he would be working on Britney Spears' new album, and he let slip that Emeli would be involved too. "There's a few tracks with William Orbit and there is also one track that Emeli wrote that will.i.am is working on," he said, before realising he might have said too much.

Perhaps a decade earlier, the concept of working with Britney would have been a dream come true for anyone wishing to raise their profile in the States. But by 2013, working with the star who shot to fame in her teenage years with 'Baby One More Time' posed an entirely different challenge. Britney's last two singles had reached 111 and 71 in the UK Singles Charts and she hoped Emeli and Naughty Boy might be able to inject some stardust back into her music.

Emeli also used her time back in London to join a panel organised by the Prince's Trust charity to help inspire young people to fulfil their ambitions. Hosted by MTV's Laura Whitmore and co-presenter AJ King, the show's panel also included *Game Of Thrones* star Ed Skrein, director and actor Adam Deacon and Radio 1 DJ Jameela Jamil, all of whom are ambassadors of the trust. Surprisingly, Emeli blamed *X Factor* for giving young people a false idea that short cuts are possible in the pursuit of dreams. Though she had benefited on several occasions from exposure on the show and related talent contests such as *America's Got Talent*, Emeli got serious in front of the sea of expectant 18 to 25-year-olds and said: "When you have things like *X Factor* it's almost showing this dream that doesn't exist: it's such a struggle getting even close to having that exposure." But she also had positive words of encouragement, telling the audience: "I think even if it feels hard at the moment, we've all been through it, we've all been working for years."

And despite all that hard work for exposure, sometimes it can have the opposite effect. Emeli was facing the beginnings of a potential backlash, as the London group Rudimental pointed out. Speaking to the *Daily Star*, the quartet revealed they had come up against what they called the "Emeli Sandé haters" – people who had attempted to dissuade them from working with her on their chart-topping debut album, *Home*. "People were telling us that maybe we shouldn't work with her as she was over-exposed, but the songs are amazing. Generally it's only the media who have created this Emeli backlash. The general public love her. You get that kind of reaction when you are successful. It's the same as any artist on our record; we didn't think about who they are or what they represent, it was about the emotion. Bottom line is her voice and the music that comes out."

For Emeli, life went on, and according to *The Sun*'s Bizarre editor, Gordon Smart, she had her eye on a new home to share with husband, Adam: a "£2.7 million pile" in Hertfordshire with seven bedrooms, a gym, wine cellar and office, which had once belonged to rock group Deep Purple.

As well as the planned UK festival appearances, Emeli returned to the States for the Outside Lands Festival in San Francisco and the Made In America Festival in Philadelphia. At Chicago's Lollapalooza festival, the singer also revealed she had been working with former Fugees star Wyclef Jean on a new EP for future release, describing the collaboration as "a dream come true". As rumours began to swirl that Emeli had co-written a song called 'It Takes Two' for Katy Perry's fourth studio album, *Prism*, she was also being linked with the BBC's number one talent show, *The Voice*. The UK's primetime reality singing contest, based on *The Voice Of Holland* created by Dutch television producer John de Mol, had become the main rival to Simon Cowell's *X Factor* franchise. The format is unique, in that it sees the judges listening with their backs to the auditioning hopefuls – focusing on the voice alone – while deciding whether to pitch to become their mentor. Jessie J, a judge on the show, alongside Welsh singing legend Tom Jones, the Script vocalist Danny O'Donoghue and hip hop artist will.i.am, planned to quit after two seasons. And the 'Do It Like A Dude' singer suggested Emeli as her replacement. "I just want someone credible and someone that can really sing, because a lot of the audience don't see the amount of work that goes in," she said. "I'd love to see someone like Emeli Sandé, Adele, Lulu, Annie Lennox."

However Emeli said she wasn't ready to pass judgement on a new generation of talent. "I feel like this is the beginning of my career. I could never go on a panel, but I'm flattered that she thought of me," she said. "I feel like maybe on my fifth album when I feel like I really know the industry, then I can go, but right now I feel like, God, you could be in the charts tomorrow and we could be competing. I feel it should be when I'm ready and I have that experience then I can impart the knowledge."

Later that month on August 25, Emeli returned to the US and attended the MTV Video Music Awards, held in New York City at

Brooklyn's newly opened Barclays Center. Again, she found herself standing shoulder to shoulder with some of the biggest celebrities on the planet. "It was amazing. The red carpet was mad to start. I was so excited to see Drake perform and Kanye [West] was amazing," Emeli enthused.

Among those who strolled down the red carpet on the night were Justin Timberlake, who walked off with four awards, Lady Gaga and fellow Brit act One Direction, who had already conquered the US in style by topping the *Billboard* charts with their first two studio albums.

October would see her return to the States where she had spent most of 2013, this time for a 12-date tour in her own right beginning in Florida and ending in Chicago. However, she still had some work to do over the pond if her guest spot on New York's Power 105.1's *Breakfast Club* show the morning after the VMAs was anything to go by. Fresh from the awards, she smiled awkwardly through an interview in which breakfast show host DJ Envy's opening gambit was to ask her how she pronounced her name. Wearing a black leather jacket, matching silk blouse and black and white gloss-painted fingernails, Emeli barely had a chance to reply before co-presenter Charlamagne Tha God, who claimed to be still drunk from the night before, asked: "First of all, who are you and what do you do? I have no clue."

Keeping it together and barely squirming, Emeli informed him that she had sold four million copies of her album back in Europe and laughed nervously before being put on the spot over Miley Cyrus' much talked about performance at the VMAs. The former Disney child star, who'd found worldwide fame as the lead in the television show *Hannah Montana*, had "twerked" her way through a duet with R&B singer Robin Thicke on his chart-topping hit 'Blurred Lines', a performance so raunchy it drew complaints from America's Parents Television Council and caused a media frenzy. "There was a lot going on," Emeli said of the 20-year-old's sexually suggestive dance routine, before being pushed to admit: "I didn't get it."

Emeli was then left speechless when DJ Envy asked: "Do you make love to your own music?"

The inquisition continued and she did her best to answer the questions put in front of her, remaining calm when Charlamagne Tha God asked: "So, what do you do? You smoke weed when you wanna get inspiration? You drink?"

"I drink, yeah," Emeli responded, getting the hang of it. "But you've got to find that place yourself. It's hard to describe. It just comes out. I don't really know the process. It just happens."

As the interview drew to a close, DJ Envy admitted that she had won him over: "I hadn't heard you, so when I heard your music today, I thought, she's dope."

Despite having to win over American DJs one at a time, the British radio and television presenter who first spotted Emeli's talent when she was just 16, Trevor Nelson, believes that her abilities as a singer and songwriter have given her something of an edge during her time in the US. And he has no doubt she'll make it just as big there. "The thing about Emeli Sandé is she is a black girl from Aberdeen and that's a bonus because people around the world probably don't think there are black people in Aberdeen," Nelson said. "When people hear her speak it's not what people expected to hear. I think it's tremendous for her and it's what makes people like Emeli slightly more interesting, particularly when they are going around the world doing promo. With Emeli Sandé, I don't think they need to ask her what makes her different from every other singer. It is summed up by seeing her perform and hearing her speak."

Nelson believes Adele Adkins helped pave the way for Emeli to shine. "Before Adele, what did people call a star? A girl in lingerie who stands there in high heels," he said. "I personally think the music industry was leaning that way for a long time. I can honestly say that with the breakthrough of Adele it changed the attitude of a lot of the record labels because it is clear Emeli Sandé will not be hanging out at the opening of nightclubs. Emeli is not a girl who cares too much about being at the height of fashion, being at the opening of an envelope or walking up a red carpet."

While the rejection she faced in the early years delayed her opportunity to reach out to her audience, Richard Blackwood insists it only made Emeli stronger. "That's great. Trust me. Getting rejected by labels is the best thing that could happen to you. Can you imagine the record labels that could have had her and how they are feeling now? The other thing is she probably wasn't ready. She had her own growing to do. If you get rejected by record companies and people don't think you're ready yet, you're not, because once you do make it and once you are successful there is no turning back because all eyes are on you. I think what's good for Emeli is that it has taken as long as it has to evolve. If she was successful back then I don't think she would be around now. She's at an age now where she is a veteran now, if you think about it. It's 10 years on, she's done many shows and perfected her craft and now she is ready for success, so I think it's good that it has happened for her at this time in her life. Right now, Emeli has won many different awards and she is established. So everything she does now is watched. Now she is embarking on America and the critics there are going to be watching her but because of those years coming up and learning her craft, she's more than ready."

Having followed in Emeli's footsteps when he won the BRITs Critics' Choice award in 2013, Tom Odell says of his predecessor: "I think she is a brilliant singer and a brilliant songwriter. It's so nice to see that kind of music doing well. It's amazing. I just spent time in America as well and there are so many British artists doing well over there. There really is a bit of a British invasion going on with Mumford & Sons, Adele and Emeli. It's great to see. There is a real excitement and buzz in British music again."

A★M★E, who had recorded Emeli's song 'Find A Boy' before also going on to enjoy chart-topping success as a featured artist, said: "She deserves it. Her album is amazing, all her singles are amazing. She has an incredible voice. She definitely has deserved it all."

Emeli's former drummer Dade Thomas is another collaborator who isn't surprised that his friend has gone on to enjoy the level of fame that has come her way. "I knew from the minute I saw her, one hundred percent. I've always backed Emeli," he said. "She was the best thing I had ever seen in Scotland. Her songwriting ability is just insane. Her voice is incredible, but her ability to communicate her music and songwriting is incredible. She deserves every bit of her success."

Looking back, Emeli admits the degree of success she has enjoyed has been unexpected. "I just made music I loved. I made an album that I was really proud of and I didn't compromise on anything. So when you do that you can't bank on commercial success, so I was really surprised."

Regarding making it as an artist in her own right, Emeli perhaps summed up the attitude that has helped her find fame against the odds when she said: "Music never stops. You can always be writing. You can always do something else. It's forever."

Index

All song titles by Emeli Sandé unless indicated otherwise.

185

Index

189